Dental Wealth

Why What You May Have Been Taught to Be True About Money Has Turned Out Not to Be

By: Sean A. Quigley LUTCF
& Bryan S. Bloom CPA

INFINITY
PUBLISHING

ISBN 978-0-7414-7879-5 Paperback
ISBN 978-0-7414-7880-1 eBook
Library of Congress Control Number: 2012945773

Printed in the United States of America

Published January 2013

INFINITY PUBLISHING
1094 New DeHaven Street, Suite 100
West Conshohocken, PA 19428-2713
Toll-free (877) BUY BOOK
Local Phone (610) 941-9999
Fax (610) 941-9959
Info@buybooksontheweb.com
www.buybooksontheweb.com

Acknowledgements

Sean:

As Bryan and I put the finishing touches on our book this week, I received the most incredible news. My wife, Elizabeth, received results of a PET Scan showing that the terminal cancer she was diagnosed with one year ago is almost entirely resolved. So, when it comes to acknowledgements, I want to give all the glory to God for her healing and for bringing us the family and friends that prayed with us for this great miracle! I wish I could name each person and all the acts of care and kindness, but I will have to do that privately with each one of you...just know that our whole family appreciates you so much and we hope to return the love in the future.

I also want to acknowledge and send out a prayer for all those that are facing challenges such as we had this year and assure them that God has a plan and sometimes emotional and physical suffering allows His love and mercy to be revealed in a way that we would have never imagined!

To Elizabeth: My wife of 18 years and the love of my life! You are so amazing and you showed incredible courage and openness to God in prayer this year. Every minute of every day is fun because of your smile, your laughter, your joy, your wit, and, of course, your silly humor which only a few of us get. Even the dogs are excited when you get home and maybe that is because you have those in depth conversations with them as if they knew what you were saying. This was a big week and we are going to keep celebrating for a year or more!

To Megan: My 14 year-old daughter and my prayer partner, who helped with the care of your mother for the past year, even learning to be her nurse and taking the needles out of her arm and bringing her what she needed. I knew it was hard for you this year, but you showed a lot of courage and you kept a smile on your face each day. You are a special girl and that smile and laughter is infectious. You, also, have the most amazing friends! They and their families have made this, our new home in Lincoln, Nebraska, come alive with all kinds of fun!

To Chad: My 15 year-old son and "best buddy", every day I look forward to the minute you get up in the morning because that is when the fun begins and it has been that way since the day you were born. You love life and you have always found the most amazing friends! You have many talents, but your greatest gift is that of humility and you demonstrate it each and every day. Your mother and I love and appreciate you so much!

To Bryan: My co-author and great friend! It has been quite a journey and many hours, days, and months of conversations, research, website design, etc., but it was all worth it and it has been so rewarding! You are incredibly intelligent and professional in your career in the financial services industry. Clearly you enjoy every minute of your work and your life with your wonderful family. I appreciate your friendship and it has truly been an honor for me to have the opportunity to work with you on this project.

There are many others to thank and I will thank you in person when I see you, but I must thank those that directly supported us and challenged us to write this book. First of all, the many clients and their families who have placed their trust in us through the years and to my fellow advisors who heard about our work and were our cheerleaders and many times offered thoughts and ideas for the book. To Don Blanton, T. Jay DiBacco, Mic Jund, Dan

Allison, Phil Cavender, Bob and Marilyn Diers, Jim Spitsen, and especially to Ray Garretson for approaching me as I walked out of the church one day and told me he thought I would do well in the financial services industry. Thanks Ray...it has been quite a ride!

Bryan:

There are so many people who have influenced my career and encouraged me to write this book, all of whom have made this book possible.

First and foremost, I am grateful to my Heavenly Father, the Yahweh of the Old Testament of the Bible who lets me call him "Abba Father" and his Son Jesus Christ who is my personal Lord and Savior.

I'd also like to thank my wife, Pam and children Callie Sederquist and Corrie Musgrave for their love and encouragement to write and create.

My extended family have been influential as well, my parents, John and Jackie Bloom, Pam's parents, Harold and Annie Jean Ray. Thank you. My first clients; my brother Jeff and Pam's sister and brother-in-law, Angela and Byron Boyd; thank you for letting me experiment on you.

None of this could have been possible without the support of my friends at Chesser Financial. My fellow financial advisors; Jamie Chesser, John Butler, Jim Lilley, Terri Wetzel, Rich Bloom, Tim Noice and Scott Olthoff. Thank you for helping edit the content of this book and for your ideas of what to include. The support staff at Chesser Financial can often go unnoticed because they do their jobs so well; but not here! Thank you Bette, Chrissy, Cassie, Eric, and Christy.

Many thanks go to two people at Chesser Financial that I could never have done without. Jason and Sarah Fagan. Jason, you have served me so well as my personal assistant that you saw the potential of helping others financially and chose to become an advisor. I consider that a compliment. Thank you for picking up so many pieces that would have fallen through the cracks without your unselfish service. Sarah, thank you for all the little things you do, that add up to huge things when I don't get them done.

I would be remiss, if I didn't mention my "study group". This group of individuals has helped me refine my thinking about what I was taught to be true. Each time I would realize another fallacy of traditional financial thinking, these guys verified my thinking. Thanks to Jamie Chesser, Jim Lilley, Rich Wesselt, Ian Meierdiercks, Phil Bodine, Phil Cavender, and John Cush.

Finally, I'd like to thank some of my friends and inspirers from within the financial services industry. When I first started my independent career, Roger Pryor was a significant encourager for me to succeed in my career. Professionally, I owe a debt of gratitude to Larry Adams, Doc Huffman and David O'Malley who presented me with the Chairman's Navigator Award in 2010 in recognition of "the highest standard of professionalism, dedication, commitment and leadership". The award presented during the 100th anniversary of The Ohio National Financial Services Company, was presented for only the second time. It is given to an individual "who is of exceptional character and integrity". Thank you for your confidence in me by granting me this honor.

Table of Contents

Foreword

Life as a Dentist

First of all, we would like to thank all the many dentists that we have worked with through the years who have encouraged us to write this book. The ideas and topics you suggested we address, will be, and we hope it helps you continue to grow and enjoy your career as a dentist and have all the personal rewards that go along with it.

Bryan and I consider it a great blessing to have had the opportunity to work with you and to witness your entrepreneurial spirit at work. You all came out of dental school with your own vision of how you wanted to develop your practice. Some chose to have a large, fast-paced environment within the city, others may have chosen a smaller practice treating patients in more rural areas, and still others have chosen to specialize. Our goal in writing this book was to reach out to all of you and contribute to your success by greatly enhancing your financial portfolio.

Have you ever heard of the "Aha!" experience... when suddenly the answer presents itself, fresh and new? No one doubts that such epiphanies exist. They can be life changing as in the so-called "peak" experience, when reality is flooded with light.

Epiphany

e·piph·a·ny - ⟦ i píffənee ⟧

noun

1. A sudden manifestation or perception of the essential nature or meaning of something.

We live in a world in which perception becomes reality in the mind of the beholder. The perception is that dentists are swimming in cash the day they graduate from dental school. Dentists are among the brightest and most successful in society, and certainly you need not worry about money after your practice is established. You can do very well financially if you are smart with your money but, as you know, it takes time and it takes years to truly build a practice to the point where the business model is running on all cylinders. A successful Dental practice has a cohesive and committed staff of professionals working alongside of you, as well.

The reality is that all this takes time. You must be open with your staff and desire their input and support in finding the path to success. Being a dentist can be the most enjoyable and rewarding profession if you live to your own expectations and find peace of mind and heart in knowing that you and your staff are committed to providing the very best dental care for your patients. The financial reward will come and you will be able to provide for you and your family. Working and living with a conservative and big picture approach will serve you, your staff, and your family well throughout your career.

When we set out together on this project, we decided that the best thing we could do for dentists was to look at their overall picture and what are the main issues that they are faced with every day. So we are going to "cut to the chase" so to speak, and show you how many of the things that we were all taught to be true by outside influences have turned out not to be so true after all. We are going to peel the layers back on the various financial traditions to demonstrate the strengths and weaknesses of each. We will take an analytical approach and reveal the truths and untruths about how money works with verifiable numbers and mathematical calculations.

"Discovery consists of seeing what everyone else has seen and thinking what nobody has thought" – Albert Szent-Györgyi

It is fascinating how each of you has your own unique approach to how you run your practice. On the other hand, there are certain financial aspects that you all have in common and most of the decisions you make directly affect your bottom line and ultimately the personal wealth you are able to accumulate. The key is to then grow that income as free from tax as possible while retaining liquidity, use, and control of your money for any life or business circumstances that may appear through the years.

We have found that if you are able to implement these truths, you may see an increase in your cash flow, your production, and your personal estate almost immediately. You will be better protected from stock market crashes or downturns in the economy. The 2008 recession was the best wake-up call this country could have had. From a business perspective as traditional lines of credit became unavailable, many businesses could not cover their cash flows and failed. Medical and dental reimbursements from the insurance industry and government have become unpredictable, at least in the short run, putting further strain on cash flows. Now it is time to get your house and dental practice in order and be prepared for similar events which may happen again during your career. We truly believe that there is more opportunity to help you financially in discovering processes to avoid the losses than trying to predict which product will outperform other products. That is what we attempt to do in the following pages.

If what you thought to be true, turned out not to be, when would you want to know? Obviously, right away...so, let's get to it!

Miracle of Compound Interest

It has been called the eighth wonder of the world. Whether you are looking at the seven wonders of the ancient world, seven wonders of the natural world or the seven wonders of the modern world, many would add the miracle of compound interest as the eighth wonder. It has risen to such heights, because the exponential curve it creates rises to heights that command our attention. It doesn't matter whether you save a single sum, or a series of amounts, when left alone to grow, it grows exponentially. When not only your deposits earn interest, but its interest earns interest as well: the potential is unlimited.

It doesn't matter whether you are saving for a child's education, your retirement years after leaving your dental practice, or even to leave a legacy from your physical lifetime, the miracle occurs. Let's consider the first two of these, since this is what I was taught to believe how it would work.

Now that you are through dental school, you are very aware of the costs associated with it. Dental school is expensive, and there is not much that can be done to defray those costs, but how you save for school is as important as saving is in the first place. Suppose you were to have a child today and wanted to begin their college savings fund immediately. In order to have a sufficient sum of money available to pay four years of public university education eighteen years from now, you would need to begin saving $9,000 each year for 18 years. If you did that you would have saved $162,000 of your own money, but your account would have grown to $265,000 if you had been able to earn 5% on that money each of the 18 years. The extra $100,000 comes from not only your money earning interest but your interest earning interest. Enough to pay over $70,000 per year for four years of junior's education. Yes, that is a lot, but it is merely today's costs of tuition for a public university compounding at 2011 increases.

At the end of the four years of education the University now has the $265,000 and you have zero. Not only does the University have the money, but they have the ability to earn interest on the money, that was once your opportunity. We call that transferring the parent's miracle to the University's miracle!

If you wanted to accumulate the magic retirement amount of $1,000,000 between your college graduation and age 65, a mere 43 years, you'd need to save less per year than you need for juniors education. In fact, at an earnings rate of the same 5%, you'd need to save $6,660 per year. Why less? Because the retirement miracle has 43 years to run, not just 18.

Let's combine these two ideas we begin to further understand this miracle. If the college funding of $9,000 were to run for 18 years and then that value continued to be allowed to earn for another 47 years instead of transferring the miracle to the university, junior would have $2,633,512 to retire on. Let's take it one last step, what if junior added his own $6,660 to mom and dad's college savings? He could retire on over 3.8 million dollars! Now do you see why it is called a miracle?

Some financial advisors would lead you to believe that you can earn more than 5%, indeed you might, and if you do, the miracle gets even better. If you can add just 1% to this last example at age 65 you would have almost $5.8 million. Many advisors still believe you can earn 8% in the market over the long run, which would yield a miraculous result of $13 million. And if you listen to a popular financial talk show host, he would tell you that you can earn 12%. If the miracle grew at the rate of 12%, which would be even more miraculous than compound interest, you would have $67 million!

If the miracle of compound interest were really true, why aren't we all rich by now? Even if you earned 8% on a $100 per month savings plan over your working career you would have $450,000 at age 65. Are you on target? If what you were taught to be true turned out not to be, when would you want to know? Keep reading.

Look at the following graph. This is $9,000 per year being saved for 18 years at 5%. Notice the graph isn't exponential.

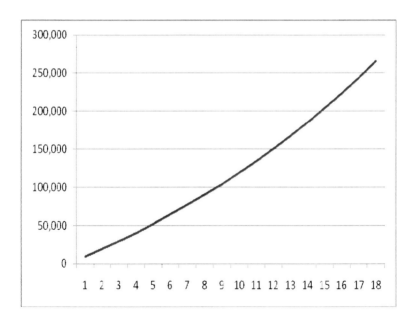

But look at the Universities graph after the money is transferred to them. Notice the linear nature of the first 18 years, and the exponential growth after the money is in the hands of the University. We are assuming the same 5% rate of return.

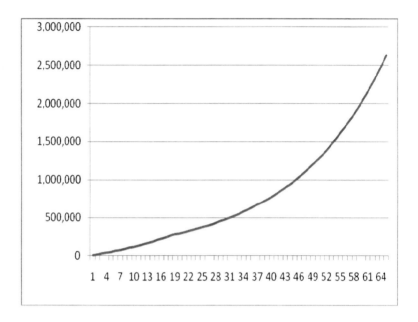

Lesson #1: Why what we were taught to be true about the miracle of compound interest that has turned out not to be true, is that there is no allowance for spending money during the compounding period. When we spend the miracle, we transfer it to someone else and the compounding stops for us.

This lesson is compounded due to taxes. Even if we don't choose to spend the miracle, we may be forced to spend some of it to pay the taxes due on the annual growth of the account. If we don't pay it from the account, we have to compromise our lifestyle to pay the income taxes. Funds to pay income taxes due on the growth have to come from somewhere, either from the account itself, or from our discretionary spending budget. If the money comes from the account, the miracle can't work, and if it comes from a compromised lifestyle, that doesn't sound like much fun.

Let's go back to the million dollar retirement. Because Uncle Sam demands that you pay taxes on the interest and dividends you earn, as you earn them, the million dollars are stunted greatly. Paying a combined federal and state tax rate of 30% on the earnings as earned, reduces your miracle to $667,000.

If you add up the tax on just the growth each year, the tax you pay is $163,000, but the miracle of compound interest is now working against you. Because the taxes due were extracted from the account, they were no longer in the account to earn the compounding interest. A dollar spent is no longer available to ever earn again and that is called opportunity cost. The opportunity cost of paying the taxes out of the account is another $170,000. Add the two together and subtract the total from the original million you thought you'd have and you end up with $667,000. Not exactly the million dollar retirement you had in mind.

As fast as the exponential curve is increasing while interest is compounding, the taxes due and the lost opportunity from paying the tax is increasing in a negative fashion. The taxes due and the lost opportunity from paying the tax is eroding the money that you had been compounding.

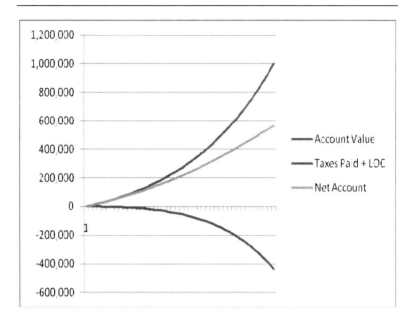

Look at the net account line as it is nearly linear again. The taxes stole your miracle.

Lesson #2: Why what we were taught to be true about compound interest that has turned out not to be true is the taxes due on the growth tarnishes the miracle by reducing the amount of money that the miracle would otherwise expect.

There is still at least one more reason why what we were taught to be true about compound interest hasn't turned out to be true. When we realize it doesn't work – we quit.

Let's use the example of someone who wants to invest $5,000 per year and actually experiences a 9% rate of return on their investments. Slowly, the account gains momentum, but by the time the exponential curve begins to take place in year 18 you realize the following:

Year	Annual Deposit	Beg. Of Year	Annual "1099"	Annual Tax Due
1	5,000	5,000	450	-135
2	5,000	10,450	941	-282
3	5,000	16,391	1,475	-443
4	5,000	22,866	2,058	-617
5	5,000	29,924	2,693	-808
6	5,000	37,617	3,386	-1,016
7	5,000	46,002	4,140	-1,242
8	5,000	55,142	4,963	-1,489
9	5,000	65,105	5,859	-1,758
10	5,000	75,965	6,837	-2,051
11	5,000	87,801	7,902	-2,371
12	5,000	100,704	9,063	-2,719
13	5,000	114,767	10,329	-3,099
14	5,000	130,096	11,709	-3,513
15	5,000	146,805	13,212	-3,964
16	5,000	165,017	14,852	-4,455
17	5,000	184,869	16,638	-4,991
18	5,000	206,507	18,586	-5,576

You get to year 18 and you realize that you are paying more in taxes annually, than you are saving annually. Why? A very good question, and you stop saving!

For those inclined to stop saving, the thinking goes like this: In the early years, it's not so bad. In year one, you are paying only an extra $135 in taxes. You hardly notice it, and perhaps it only reduces your tax refund at the end of the year. The year two taxes are only $147 more than in year one, and again you don't

7

notice. It is like having the heat slowly being turned up, the cold water warms, it grows in temperature, it eventually gets hot, and before you know it your goose is cooked and what you are saving is being spent on taxes! As the chart shows, your account is worth over $200,000, but it is costing you more in taxes than what you are depositing each year.

Lesson #3: Why what we were taught to be true that has turned out not to be true about compound interest is that when we realize the impact of having to pay taxes on the growth of our account we may stop saving or investing.

Rate of Return

In speaking with our dental clients, the subject of "rate of return" comes up quite regularly. Many of you ask why the balances on your investment statements don't seem to reflect the stated average rate of return. We need to analyze the numbers if we truly want to understand where they are coming from and truly learn how those numbers are calculated.

What is average? An average is something common or typical. When used to describe a rate of return it is what can be expected to happen over and over again, resulting in a hypothetical projection. The expectation of the future is often based on the history of the past, even though every investment projection you see states that "past performance is not a prediction of future performance". A common way of looking at average is to calculate the mean of a series of numbers. The mean return over a number of years is the sum of the returns during those specific years divided by the number of years you are looking at. This number is commonly referred to as the average rate of return. However you define "average", what I've learned is that what I've been taught about averages couldn't be further from the actual truth.

Let's start with a fairly simple example. If you had $1,000 and averaged 20% per year for two years, you would have $1,440 at the conclusion of two years.

An average rate of return is an easy and convenient way to project the future potential of a financial plan. Too bad it doesn't work. The main reason why average rates of return are a faulty way of looking at your finances is because averages are not actual rates of return and the order in which actual returns occur can make a big difference.

Take for example the S&P 500 index for the period 1973 through 1997. During this 25 year time period the S&P suffered through some of its worst periods of time including a single day drop of over 22% in 1987 and one of its longest rallies during the 1990's. During this time period the index had an average annual rate of return of 10.11%. Indeed, if you added up each individual annual return and divided by 25 you would arrive at the statistical average of 10.11%.
Source: www.standardandpoors.com

If you invested $100,000 in 1973 and actually earned 10.11% each year for twenty five years you would have the expectation that your nest egg would be $1,110,000. Unfortunately, you don't earn the same rate each year, so let's calculate what you would have really had at the conclusion of those 25 years had you invested $100,000 in 1973 and earned what the market actually earned year after year. If you had left it to grow and compound, you would have $821,000. This is a difference of $279,000 less than the average would have created!

Lesson #1: Why what we were taught to be true that turned out not to be about rates of return is that averages aren't what you actually get to spend and enjoy.

From what we learned in chapter 1; what hasn't been accounted for yet? That's right - taxes. Average rates of return, in fact actual returns as well, are never reduced for taxes when they are disclosed to you. Those typical mountain charts that you are provided with every time you purchase a mutual fund assumes you are paying the taxes on the growth of the fund from your lifestyle.

What if the taxes due were netted out of the account instead of out of your standard of living? Let's consider a hypothetical mutual fund with a 76 year history. Without netting the taxes out of the fund balance their marketing piece would show that $10,000 invested in their fund in 1934 would grow to almost $58.5 million dollars if you reinvested the dividends paid by the fund. Rarely, would the fund marketing material indicate that the taxes due each year on the growth of the fund are paid by the investors "other" money to make the numbers and graph work. If you netted the taxes from the fund, assumed to be 30% of the fund's income return and 15% of its capital gain return, your $10,000 investment 76 years ago, would be just shy of $8.9 million. That is 84% less than what you are lead to believe from the fund's growth chart.

Lesson #2: Why what we were taught to be true has turned out not to be about rates of return is that taxes take a large portion of my expectations away.

Now that you have a good feel for why what we are taught about rates of return aren't necessarily true, let's finish with the fairly simple example we started with. By now, you are probably thinking that what seems to be simple may not be. Our example was an investment of $1,000 that averages 20% over 2 years would yield $1,440. But might it also yield:

$1,280? It sure will. An extremely volatile market that earns 60% in the first year and then loses 20% the second year has an average rate of return of 20%, and an account value of $1,280, not $1,440.

11

$800? Of course not, how can you average a positive rate of return and end up with less money? There once was a time, not too many years ago that you could purchase an un-built home and sell it for twice what you paid for it before you moved in. That is a 100% return. Shortly, thereafter, that same property fell 60% in value. Over the two year period the average rate of return was 20%, yet you have less money.

$0? Now you know this is a trick question, but again it is true. You can average 20% for two years and yet lose all of your money. Anyone who earns 140% and then loses it all – 100%, ends up with $0 yet averaged 20%.

Lesson #3: Why what we were taught to be true about rates of return and has turned out not to be is that how much money you end up with is more important than any rate of return. Advertised or stated rates have been far different than what most of our dental clients have actually experienced in their portfolio. We have pointed out more than once that the growth in their fund balance, especially in the past several years, has been mostly the contributions they have made to the fund from their dental practice and not necessarily from growth within the fund itself.

Paper Gains

You may have a friend or have overheard someone in a crowd tell everyone about their trip to Las Vegas and how they hit the $16,000 jackpot! It was awesome!

Everybody is just fascinated and wishes they had been there to experience the thrill, right? Sure, it is exciting and no wonder they are building casinos all over the country so more and more people can experience the same "high", so to speak.

Many of you have experienced those same "highs" when you open up your quarterly investment statement. We've already shown you how they calculate those numbers, but what I hope you get out of this discussion is the fact that you had no gain or loss at all because you didn't cash out at the time you received the statement. We call those "paper gains" because those gains are worth no more than the paper they were printed on unless you call up your stock broker or financial advisor and have them move that money out and realize those gains. In all actuality, those probably were not truly gains if you consider that the market hasn't even recovered the losses sustained in 2008.

Do you ever wonder why they send you a statement showing you how much money is in your IRA or 401(k)? If you can't take it out without penalties until your 59 ½ anyway, does it matter how much is in there when you're 35? It may be worth less at age 59 ½ than it is worth now, so why bother?

The same goes for real estate, or precious metals, or wherever the flavor of the week "jackpot" happens to be that quarter. We all remember when everyone supposedly had double or triple the price they had paid for their home and couldn't find a contractor to build the new wing onto their home because they were all busy building second and third homes next to the ski resort for their neighbors...paper gains.

There are companies spending fortunes advertising gold and silver as the next "jackpot" just waiting to be taken by the highest bidder. Even though you may have those shiny little coins locked up in your safe in the basement, the metal is only worth the price on the paper advertising the latest bid price.

Lesson #1: Why what we were taught to be true about our investment statements, our gold bricks, or our house that has turned out not to be true is that when you hear that someone, somewhere, somehow, sold their house for that unbelievable price... that must mean yours is worth that much, as well. You may also find out that when you decide it is time to cash out, your gold or your 401(k) have very little value and, by the way, the gains have not yet been taxed.

The only time any of these paper gains are true gains is when you cash them out. This is why we need to be sure that the profits from your dental practice are put into an account that will grow consistently and not be affected by these cycles in the various markets.

Lesson #2: Why what we were taught to be true about paper gains that has turned out not to be true is that paper gains have no purchasing power at all. They lead to a false sense of security as lifestyle and business purchases are based on the paper gain, not the actual economic value of the realizable gains. During the stock market boom of the 1980's and 1990's, many transferred safe funds to the market to participate in these gains. Consumer and business purchases were made along the way without a responsible transfer of the paper gains back to safe money, only to see the paper gains disappear in the early 2000's and again in 2008. If you are going to participate in the market's paper gains, you must systematically and responsibly make the paper gains, realized gains.

So, your goal should be to grow your practice and build liquidity as soon as possible so you don't have to worry so much about economic downturns. More importantly, you need to be sure that the day you decide to retire that the money you have accumulated is in a cash account that is out-pacing inflation and is truly worth the number printed on that piece of paper.

Financing Large Purchases

How you buy things may be the key to the success of your dental practice. Many of the dentists that we work with are used to going to the bank or financial services broker for loans to make purchases for their practice such as new computers and practice management software, or for new digital cameras, and equipment. This is an acceptable strategy if you already have a private reserve established which would give you the flexibility of paying off that structured loan at a moment's notice while maintaining the compounding effect on your money.

Every purchase large or small is a financing decision. As described in previous chapters, it is not just interest charged on a purchase when you purchase with credit, but also interest not earned if you use your own money.

What if you were the bank?

If you have any savings at all, you are the bank, but you just don't know it. And because you don't know it, you don't treat yourself as a bank. If you treated yourself as a bank, you would pay yourself back for every purchase you made. That is not feasible, which is why we need to segment out purchases for consumption from purchases and expenses of larger items such as a new CAD/CAM system for your practice, a dental chair, vehicles, college educations, homes, real estate and vacations.

The list of pay yourself back purchases is personal and has infinite possibilities.

There are two keys to financial freedom and are both related to your purchasing mentality.

Every time you make a purchase from your savings, pay yourself back.

Every time you have finished paying yourself back, keep paying yourself. Somehow, you figured how your new monthly payment fit into your budget – just don't stop it, save it.

Let's first consider traditional bank financing, more specifically, financing a large purchase such as a car. When you purchase a car and you use traditional financing, you have the choice of using your bank or credit union or the convenience of the dealerships financing options. Timing is the problem with bank financing. You have to first negotiate the purchase price of the car, then at another location negotiate the terms of your loan and then bring the two together.

Many vehicle purchasers opt for the financing at the car dealership. Often times, the bank is not even considered because the interest rate at the dealership is so low. In many circumstances you can find 1.9% or 2.9% financing rates. Sometimes you can even find a 0% loan. That is like free money! These are a close cousin to the 3 years "same as cash" offers you find when your purchase furniture. The only difference is that the "same as cash" requires no payments until just before the term is over, and heaven forbid you are a day late with your payment – all the interest that accrued during the three years would be due. The 0% from the car dealership requires monthly payments.

The requirement of monthly payments is the first problem with the 0% loans. While the interest rate might be 0%, it still obligates you to a monthly payment you might not be able to afford. I have worked with plenty of people who bought more car than they should have because the loan was "free".

Have you ever wondered why a car dealership can offer 0%? They can because 0% is often not 0%. Sometimes the 0% loan is the most profitable part of the new car purchase for the car dealership.

The small print of the 0% loan discloses that if you would rather not have the 0% loan, the dealership can offer you "cash back". A good example would be the purchase of a $30,000 car at 0% or $4,000 cash back.

The payment associated with financing $30,000 at 0% for 4 years would be $625 per month for 48 months. If you paid cash using your own personal bank, what is the real purchase price of the car? What is the amount of money you would need to give the car dealership when you take delivery of the car? They would require the $30,000 less the $4,000 cash back. The real price of the car would be $26,000. If you financed yourself over the same time period at 0%, your payment to yourself would be $542 per month. So for the same car, the car dealership is charging you over 15% more. This is because the car dealership isn't really loaning the money. They typically must prepay the financing incentive to the actual lending institution in order that it can offer the 0% loan. They build the financing incentive into the higher price of the car. While there are other fees and charges that factor into the make-up of the 0% loan and higher purchase price for the car, another way to think about it is that the "cash back" you do not get when you choose the 0% loan is simply prepaid interest.

Lesson #1: Why what we were taught to be true about large purchase financing that has turned out not to be true is that 0% is not 0% when it costs us more money.

Once again we are tricked by percentages, when we ought to be paying attention to our cash flows.

The next question is: Why do you finance the entire car when you don't consume the entire car? Why does the car dealership want to be repaid the entire $30,000 by the end of the 4th year when the car may still have 50% of its value? It is because you are financing a purchase and not financing an asset.

If you were your own bank, couldn't you establish your own rules and require a repayment of only the value of the car you used during the given time frame. Of course you can. Assuming the car will still have $11,000 of value four years later, shouldn't you be paying back only $15,000? Paying yourself back $15,000 over 4 years even at an 8% rate, your car payment to yourself would be $363. That is 42% less per month than what the car dealership is going to collect if you took the 0% loan, and, you get to keep the interest. Can you think of any use you might have for $262 per month? $262 per month invested or saved at 5% for a 35 year old until retirement 30 years later is almost $219,000 toward your retirement nest egg, as long as you found a suitable tax-free investment.

If you utilize the two keys to secure financial freedom stated above, this becomes real money and actual money in your pocket.

Lesson #2: Why what we were taught to be true about large purchase financing that has turned out not to be true is that you don't have to make monthly payments for the entire purchase price, but only the portion you actually use, as long as you use yourself as a bank.

19

In the car example, you have restored $15,000 of the car value you used, and you still have a used car worth $11,000. Trade in the used car and couple that with another loan from yourself for $15,000 and purchase another $30,000 car ($30,000 less $4,000 cash back).

If you keep the discipline of saving an otherwise unnecessary monthly payment (because the loan was paid off) when you purchase the next car, you will be saving another $262 per month for 26 years at 5% you will have another $168,000 for your retirement, as long as you found another tax free investment or savings vehicle.

Lesson #3: Why what we were taught to be true about large purchase financing that has turned out not to be true is that all consumer debt is bad debt. Not when you are the bank and treat yourself like the bank!

Be a Long-Term Investor

A second cousin to the average rate of return that we have learned is to be a long term investor. If you are a long term investor you can ignore the day to day volatility of the market. Stock market history shows that the market has a long term upward slope of increasing returns. We are often pointed to the mountain charts discussed in the previous chapter.

The history of the S&P 500 proves this well. Just look at the following long term average rates of return:

1941 – 2010	12.53	a 70 year average
1951 – 2010	12.23	
1961 – 2010	11.15	
1971 – 2010	11.70	
1981 – 2010	12.18	
1991 – 2010	11.01	
2001 - 2010	3.63	

(*Source:* www.standardandpoors.com)

So as long as you are looking at a time span of around 20 years or more you will eventually get an average 11-12% on your money. Reducing these averages because average is not what you get, but actual year to year returns, you can still amass a small fortune in the long term as long as you pay the taxes from your lifestyle.

However, these are not the returns that the average investor receives. The 2011 Dalbar Study of Investor Returns, found that over the last 20 years when the S&P 500 returned an average of 9.14%, the average equity investor earned just 3.83%. Source: www.dalbar.com

Why is that? Part of it is investment selection, but most of the difference is allocated to investor behavior. They just don't buy and hold for the long term. They tend to get in the market near its high. Because as the market is going up, it seems safe. Part of it is also that they don't want to be left out of the party, so they join their friends and invest. Alan Greenspan, former Federal Reserve Chairman, has referred to this as irrational exuberance. Then when the market corrects, they exercise some control and stay in, understanding that they are a long term investor. Then, they begin to see others get out of the market, they start to lose sleep, and they sell near the bottom of the correction. Then, as the market begins to recover, they wait, they vow they aren't going to be caught by a "suckers rally", wait a little more, make sure the market is really back on the upward climb and they get back in. They literally buy high and sell low! The human psyche is just more fragile than the computer models that can calculate the long term rates of return we all ought to be getting if we were just patient.

Notice also that the long term is a long time. The money has to be in the market to get these returns. Not only can't you chicken out, you can't spend the money – not even for taxes.

Lesson #1: Why what we were taught to be true about being a long term investor that has turned out not to be true is that being a long term investor requires a discipline or stubbornness that human behavior pattern's rarely allow.

Bryan's daughter, a graduate of one of the most highly rated public universities in America started her career in finance a few years ago. She started her career just in time to see the stock market fall by 40% and then quickly rebound by 50%. She called on the phone and told Bryan that she had a training presentation to give and she just couldn't get the numbers to work out, and would he help her. She explained that she wanted to show how well the market recovered from its recent collapse. She used the example of $100,000 invested in this volatile 40% down and 50% up market. She quickly discovered that what she was taught to be true turned out not to be. Rates of return are not additive. And even though the premise of the previous chapter on averages would lead you to believe that over the two year period of time you had earned 10% total, 5% average, it wasn't just not true, it wasn't even close.

$100,000
less 40%   the market "correction"
$60,000
Plus 50%   the market "recovery"
=$90,000

Bryan confirmed with her that her numbers were right and instead of earning an average 5% over the two year period, she actually lost an average 5% per year.

Then she made a remarkable statement. She said; "just think if you didn't lose money. If the 40% loss could have just been a breakeven year, and then even if I just earned half of what the market earned the next year, I'd have $125,000."

Let's see how our long term rates of return would have fared if we could eliminate all the negatives, replace them with zeros and take just 75% of the positives. For each of the following time periods below you would have the stated rate of return over and above what staying in the market for the long term would have yielded:

1931 – 2010	166%	in other words you would have 166% more money if you eliminated the negatives and replaced the positives with 75% of the actual return.
1941 – 2010	1%	
1951 – 2010	13%	
1961 – 2010	43%	
1971 – 2010	32%	
1981 – 2010	8%	
1991 – 2010	37%	
2001 - 2010	84%	

(*Source:* www.standardandpoors.com)

Here is another way to look at this. If you invested $10,000 at the beginning of each of these periods, by eliminating the negatives of the stock market, but only taking 75% of the gain when the market went up your investment nest egg would be higher in every time period.

	All the return	Eliminating the losses	More money	% More
1931–2010	16,608,401	44,191,632	27,583,231	166
1941–2010	15,022,156	15,228,921	206,765	1
1951–2010	4,545,666	5,120,715	575,049	13
1961–2010	1,020,396	1,458,875	438,479	43
1971–2010	486,953	644,162	175,578	37
1981–2010	210,575	228,135	17,560	8
1991–2010	57,504	78,865	21,361	37
2001–2010	11,505	21,166	9,661	85

This table illustrates that small advantages can mean a lot of money in real terms. For instance, the advantage of limiting the gains to only 75% in exchange for eliminating all the losses is only a 1% difference in the time period 1941-2010, which doesn't sound like much. But that is a real dollar advantage of over $200,000.

For the longest time period 1931-2010, you would have needed to exchange the negatives for only 2/3rds of the positives to break even. But remember, human behavior may have caused the investor to have, at times, deviated from being a long term investor, or may have spent some of the money.

Lesson #2: Why what we were taught to be true about being a long term investor that has turned out not to be true is that taking the losses with the gains is a losing strategy. Limit your losses even at the expense of some of your gains.

One of the longest standing traditional investment strategies is "dollar cost averaging", that is, getting into the market a little at a time. If you invest the same amount of money as the market is going up, your invested total grows as you add money, you merely purchase fewer, more valuable individual shares. However, you limit your upside potential since you didn't buy all at once at the low price. But at the same time, you are protecting your available investment dollars should the market move expectantly down.

If the market heads lower, you still invest the same amount of money, but you buy more shares at a lower price. You are never buying all of your position either high or low. "Dollar Cost Averaging" helps keep you disciplined to stay in the declining market, because you are systematically buying more less-expensive shares. You continue to buy and to stay in. Seems to me if I just don't lose money in the market as illustrated earlier, in exchange for part of the upside, I'll sleep better at night.

Rarely, is it spoken to "dollar cost average" out of the market. If you take a look at the 10 years 1999-2008 you find that you would have been better off taking principle out during the downturn (limiting your loss of principle) and taking gains out during the upturn (protecting what the market gave you). Here is a simple example of removing 5% of your initial investment over this 10 year period of time.

This first chart is a chart of results had you left the money in the market over the entire period of time (source: www.standardandpoors.com). An initial investment of $100,000 would have been worth $73,461 ten years later.

	Rate of return	Beginning of the year	Gain/loss	End of the year
1999	19.51%	100,000	19,510	119,510
2000	-10.14%	119,510	-12,118	107,392
2001	-13.04%	107,392	-14,004	93,388
2002	-23.37%	93,388	-21,825	71,563
2003	26.38%	71,563	18,878	90,441
2004	8.99%	90,441	8,131	98,572
2005	3.00%	98,572	2,957	101,529
2006	13.62%	101,529	13,828	115,358
2007	3.53%	115,358	4,072	119,430
2008	-38.49%	119,430	-45,968	73,461

What if you had exercised the strategy of dollar cost averaging yourself out of the market as outlined above and removed 5% of the original investment ($5,000) each year? The growth chart would look like this:

	Withdrawal	Rate of return	Beginning of the year	Gain/loss	End of the year
1999	-5,000	19.51%	95,000	18,535	113,535
2000	-5,000	-10.14%	108,535	-11,005	97,529
2001	-5,000	-13.04%	92,529	-12,066	80,463
2002	-5,000	-23.37%	75,463	-17,636	57,828
2003	-5,000	26.38%	52,828	13,936	66,763
2004	-5,000	8.99%	61,763	5,553	67,316
2005	-5,000	3.00%	62,316	1,869	64,185
2006	-5,000	13.62%	59,185	8,061	67,247
2007	-5,000	3.53%	62,247	2,197	64,444
2008	-5,000	-38.49%	59,444	-22,880	36,564

By stripping off a percentage of the account each year you would end up with $36,564 plus the $50,000 you stripped off resulting in a total of $86,564. If you had just left the money in the account because you are a long term investor you would have $73,461, a difference of $13,103. This difference assumes you stuck the $5,000 into a mattress for safe keeping. Perhaps the money ought to land in an account that can be safe, secure and tax-free to avoid the pitfalls of traditional CPA thinking we have already discovered.

Lesson #3: Why what we were taught to be true about being a long term investor that has turned out not to be true is that leaving all your eggs in one basket taking the downs with the ups may not be any better than systematically removing risk from your investments by retreating to tax-free safety.

Qualified Plans

"There are two systems of taxation in this country... one for the informed and one for the uninformed." -Judge Learned Hand

Although many of you do not provide qualified plans for your staff, you have either personally contributed to a qualified plan or have a spouse that has an opportunity to contribute to a plan at their place of employment. Since being introduced in the 1980s, these plans have become the focus of so many of this generations' retirement portfolio, as well as, the focus of the government in regards to future taxation.

So, let's take a closer look at these plans. A qualified plan is any arrangement in which the government provides a tax deduction for making an investment and allows the growth in the account to be tax-deferred. A qualified plan is commonly known as a, 401(k), 403(b), 457, or SEP plan. Not only do you get the miracle of compound interest working in your favor, but you don't have to pay the tax -- until you take the money out of the plan.

All of these plans are provided by the employer and offer a vast but limited array of investment choices, anywhere from aggressive growth funds to stable value funds. The funds allowed for investment by the employer must include investment choices spread out over the spectrum of risk; however, you are not required to put a set amount in any one fund. The money you put into one of these employer plans is always yours, but sometimes you must meet certain criteria to actually access your money. Some of those requirements may include attaining a certain age, terminating your employment, or suffering a government defined hardship.

Some employer's sweeten the pot for you to participate. The enticement sounds like this: "if you put your money in, we (the employer) will put some in as well." The amount put in by the employer is defined by the employer, subject to Government mandated testing for discrimination against the lower paid employees, and may be subject to certain criteria. Some of these requirements include working a certain number of minimum hours each year or being employed on the last day of the year. Most of the time employer contributions are subject to a vesting schedule, so if you don't stay employed, all or a portion of the employer contributions made to your account are forfeited. The money the employer puts into the plan is tax-deductible for the employer, much like general compensation is, and is allowed to grow tax-deferred. Because the employer receives a tax deduction and it grows tax-deferred, all of the money is taxable to the employee when it is withdrawn.

An IRA is an individual retirement account which you can set up for yourself if you are not a member of an employer qualified plan. You get a tax deduction for the money you put in, and it grows tax-deferred. There are methods to consolidate IRA accounts with employer qualified plans when the employer money is made available to you through a process called a trustee to trustee transfer or rollover. Investments opportunities available in an IRA are virtually limitless.

What makes these arrangements so attractive is,

1. You don't have to pay current income taxes on the money as it goes in, nor do you have to pay current income taxes on the growth of the money each year.

2. You are investing by "dollar cost averaging", buying more shares when the price of the investment is low and buying fewer shares when the price is high, consequently averaging out the cost of participating in the plan.

3. You are taking advantage of the miracle of compound interest. Because this is a retirement plan, it is based on a lifetime of working, theoretically 30 years or more. From a previous chapter we've learned that it takes time for the miracle to take shape, so it has a real possibility to work in this situation.

4. Your investment is being made as a payroll deduction; therefore, you hardly notice the money is gone. What you don't see, you don't spend and you are saving for your retirement systematically.

We are taught to save for retirement systematically, because a little sacrifice now will provide a great benefit later. If you can get your employer to kick in some money, that is like getting a free rate of return. Because it grows tax-deferred (although it is sometimes described as tax-free), it becomes a powerful retirement savings tool. A qualified plan is one of the most explosive accumulation tools available to most employees.

It is hard to argue with all of these benefits; however it is these very advantages that contribute to making these plans erosive to your wealth when you need it the most, in your retirement years. When you begin to peel back the layers, like an onion, it begins to smell! You discover that what we have been taught to be true isn't true at all, and may be one of the worst hoaxes ever perpetrated on the American worker.

Let's see what we were taught to be true about qualified plans that we have discovered over years of practical experience, isn't true.

First, we were taught that we were saving taxes, by putting money into a qualified plan.

If you were to go to the bank and ask the banker for a loan, and he said your loan was approved, what two questions would you want an answer to before you accepted the money? You would want to know what interest rate the bank was going to charge and when they wanted the money back. What if the banker told you that at the present time the bank had plenty of money and didn't need the money back right away? In fact, you could keep the money until they needed it and at that point they would determine the interest rate. Would you take their money? Of course not!

That bank loan example is similar to what we are doing when we participate in a tax-deferred qualified plan. The IRS is due the income taxes on the income we earn with a few exceptions. One of the exceptions is money we put into a qualified plan. The taxes that would otherwise be due on the money we put into the qualified plan is deferred to some uncertain time. For the most part we are in charge of when we pay these taxes, as we use the qualified plan money as income in retirement, but the IRS demands that we begin paying the taxes at age 70 ½. Could the IRS change the required minimum distribution age? Sure they could. The taxes we defer is similar to taking a loan from the IRS for money they are otherwise due today, and agree to pay it back according to their schedule and at the income tax rate in effect at that time. Could the IRS forgive the tax "loan"? Sure they could. Could they assess a tax rate higher or lower than the tax rate that was in effect when the taxes were deferred? Sure they could. Could they assess a "success" tax on qualified plan balances over a certain amount that they might believe to be excessive? Sure they could. Which do you think is a more likely outcome? Tax forgiveness? A higher future tax rate? An excise tax? When we participate in a qualified plan we are agreeing to paying these taxes otherwise due today at some uncertain date at some uncertain rate. Would you agree to that with your banker?

Lesson #1: Why what we were taught to be true about qualified plans that has turned out not to be true is that qualified plans do not save taxes; they merely defer the tax to some uncertain date at some uncertain rate. Qualified plans do not avoid income taxes; they merely put them off to the future.

OK, so we defer the tax, what is the big deal? It is just a word. "If I put $5,000 into a deductible IRA and I'm in the 25% tax bracket, I save, I mean defer $1,250. I will just pay it later, because I can earn interest on the $1,250 I don't pay today." Let's think about that.

If this were your plan for 30 years, you would have put aside $150,000, and you would have deferred $37,500 of income taxes. If that account were invested and received an average 8% return each year, your retirement account would be worth $611,729. If you chose to supplement your other retirement income with this money for 20 years in retirement, at 8% you could withdraw $54,338 per year before you would run out of money. See what we mean about being taught that this is one of the most explosive accumulation tools of all time? If you start paying the $1,250 taxes deferred each year when you were adding money to the account, you would net out $53,088. That is still a large sum of money to supplement my other retirement income.

But it doesn't work that way! You don't just pay back what you deferred, you pay back an amount equal to the tax rate in the year you withdraw it, and assessed against the entire amount you withdraw. If you are still in the 25% tax bracket (which way do you think taxes are headed in the future?), your annual tax bill will be $13,597 each year for 20 years. That is $271,940 in taxes paid during your withdrawal years. So much for saving taxes! In fact, the taxes saved of $37,500, is paid in less than three years of retirement. Even though you have paid the government all the taxes deferred from your contributions, you get to keep paying them to cover all the taxes deferred on what your investment earned, until your qualified plan account is exhausted.

To add insult to injury, if you withdraw an amount in excess of a government mandated amount, your withdrawal will subject your social security payments to income taxes. If you can stay under the amount the government says you can have, your social security would be tax-free. It makes you wonder who owns these accounts!

Some choose to leave the money in the qualified plan and not use it. You can't do that either! The government wants its money! Beginning at age 70 ½ they tell you -- no you are supposed to know, the amount you have to take out each year. If you don't get it right, then they will tell you what you should have taken out and will assess the income tax due on what you should have taken out and add 50% of what should have been taken out as a penalty. That doesn't leave much for you!

Some choose to take out only what they have to and leave the rest for the kids at their death. That doesn't work either; your children get to pay the tax. Uncle Sam always gets his money.

When we leave a qualified plan as an inheritance, we not only leave the account value as an inheritance but also a tax bill. Thanks mom and dad!

Lesson #2: Why what we were taught to be true about qualified plans that has turned out not to be true is that while some describe these arrangements as tax-free because you don't pay the current income taxes on the amount put into the plan, they are far from tax-free. As your account compounds so do your income taxes.

Another lesson in the above example is that not only do qualified plans defer the tax, but they also defer the tax calculation. The tax rate you would have paid had you not participated in the qualified plan may or may not be the rate upon which you will pay your taxes when the taxes are due. Ask yourself, "Do I think tax rates are going to go up in the future, will go down in the future, or stay the same?" Consider, that "social security is going broke", "Medicare needs to be fixed", "the Pension Benefit Guaranty Corporation is out of money". Not only is there pressure for general income tax brackets to go up, but your personal income tax rate goes up as well because you most likely:

- have paid off your home mortgage, consequently, losing the tax deduction associated with home mortgage interest,

- your children have exceeded the age at which you receive a child tax credit

- by the time you are retired your children are no longer dependents and no longer qualified for personal exemptions on your tax return.

Lesson #3: Why what we were taught to be true about qualified plans that has turned out not to be true is that qualified plans not only defer the taxes, but they defer the tax calculation. You will pay taxes at whatever the tax rate is at the time you have to pay the tax.

You may have also been taught that you will retire in a lower tax bracket than when you were working. That might be true if you are saving for retirement truly tax-free, but as discussed, these qualified plans are anything but tax-free. If all of your retirement income will come from a tax-deferred source like a qualified plan, a successful retirement means that you are merely trading your taxable paycheck for a taxable IRA distribution.

Another principle we were taught was that you can retire on 70% of your preretirement income.

Lesson #4 and #5: Why what we were taught to be true about qualified plans that has turned out not to be true is that you most probably will not retire in a lower tax bracket, and we have yet to see anyone able to live on 70% of what they can't live on today anyway. To be comfortable in retirement you have to have complete replacement of your pre-retirement income.

The last lesson about qualified plans we are going to talk about is ownership. Just because your name is on your quarterly plan statement doesn't mean that the money is yours. First, you have to meet the vesting requirements of your employer to claim ownership of the employer's matching contributions. Even after that, the account is not yours. Because of the uncertainties of taxation, the government has first claim on your account. After the taxes are paid, at whatever the rate is in the future, the rest is finally yours. Could the government raise the tax rate in the future? Could they raise the tax on just qualified plans to something greater than the normal tax rate? Could they reinstate the old excess withdrawal tax, or institute a windfall elimination tax on qualified plans? I'll leave the answer to you, but why chance it?

Lesson #6: Why what we were taught to be true about qualified plans that has turned out not to be true is that the government has the first claim on the distributions from my qualified plan, and you get the portion they don't take away in taxes first. We now realize that it truly is like making a "deal with the devil" if, in the end, what you thought you were saving in taxes to begin with turned out to be an empty promise and you ultimately lose a large portion of your dream to higher taxes during your retirement years. If you are making any kind of income in your practice or expect to have a healthy income in your retirement years, the IRS already has a target on your back as they can see that windfall coming by reading your tax return each year.

So, for those of you that have an existing SEP, SIMPLE IRA, or 401K in your dental practice, it is never too late to make the change and improve the retirement outlook for yourself and your staff. These lessons learned now will help you and your staff avoid the government windfall tax that may be coming and, at the same time, a possible stock market downturn which has already happened to many of those that had retired prior to 2008.

Buy Term and Invest the Rest

We have all heard this phrase and it is worth taking the time to take a thoughtful look at in terms of what the words might mean when it comes to a succession plan for your dental practice or for your family. There are many philosophies or ideas pertaining to life insurance and many times these catchy phrases play a part in how we ultimately make financial decisions. It may be wise to reflect on what these words mean to us and how they will affect your strategy regarding buy/sell planning, key person insurance, or cash accumulation for your dental practice.

Life insurance is often considered a necessary evil. Something you pay for and never receive anything for it. Life insurance is designed to help a family or business financially if the income earner meets with an early demise. The question we have to ask ourselves is what would our spouse and our children do if I were to die? Also, what would happen to my dental practice which would directly impact my family, my staff, and my patients? In this sense, life insurance ought to be labeled death insurance.

Let's first look at it from the perspective of how it would affect your own family. Some might say "my spouse will remarry"; others will say he/she will get a job, or second job. Others will say, if I buy enough life insurance he/she will not have to do either, my family will move ahead without me or a financial hardship.

Before we address the buy term insurance and invest the rest, let us address these first two solutions.

If you say, my spouse will remarry, have you ever had that conversation before it became your conclusion? If not, we'd suggest you do. If your spouse remarries, what would you want for him or her? Would you like the second marriage to be for love or for money? It sure is a lot easier when financial concerns can be removed from the remarriage question, and the answer can come from the same perspective in which you married – for love!

Lesson #1: Why what we were taught to be true about not needing life insurance that has turned out not to be true is that if it is ever my spouse's desire to remarry after my death, I want it to be out of love, not because of the need for money.

If you say my spouse will get a job, have you ever considered why your spouse isn't working now? If it is for the consideration of child rearing, does the dream of mom or dad staying home with kids change just because someone has died? I would think not. During the period of dating and engagement, many dreams are constructed. After marriage, these dreams are begun and carried out over a lifetime. Life insurance is the only thing that can insure that the dreams of our early years really do come true. So life insurance isn't really a necessary evil – life insurance is a dream realizer. The necessary evil is paying for it.

Lesson #2: Why what we were taught to be true about not needing life insurance that has turned out not to be true is that if my spouse ever has to face the future without me (or my income) I don't want it to have to change all the hopes and dreams we had together. I don't want her to have to work if she doesn't want to. I still want my children to go to the college of their choice and not settle for something more affordable that doesn't

39

offer the curriculum that they would like to pursue, or not attain a college degree at all.

Before we can calculate the cost of life insurance we must first calculate how much death benefit is necessary. Consider a wage earner earning $100,000 a year. This is a good amount to consider because it is easily scalable, if you earn $200,000 just double the calculations and so on. If a spouse needed to replace $100,000 per year, and he/she could earn 5% consistently and safely, a nest egg of $2,000,000 is necessary. Some would consider this nest egg the deceased's human life value, but it falls short when you account for what the future may hold. All this amount means is that the family could continue to live at the same standard of living as they did without the need to generate the lost wage through trading the family's time for money. That is twenty times income and for many insurance companies stretches the upper limits of what they will provide. This ignores the likelihood of earning 5% every year, the family need for periodic lump sums like cars, vacations, college educations and weddings. Add these to the mix and the answer to what the deceased's human life value is better defined: as much as the insurance company is willing to provide.

Lesson #3: Why what we were taught to be true about buy term and invest the rest is that there is no sum of money that an insurance company will issue that can fund the hopes and desires that my family and I ever dreamt about.

Term life insurance can be purchased in various ways, either with an annual premium amount that increases with age, or a premium that stays level for a certain period of time and then increases after that with age. At a certain point the annual increases in cost are prohibitive, but that is designed to happen after the children are grown, through college and on their own, otherwise known as "off the family payroll!" It is now mom and dad in their retirement years without the "need" for life insurance and therefore when it gets too expensive they just drop the life insurance policy and consider themselves "self-insured". They become "self-insured" because during that same time period they accumulated a nest egg equal to the amount of term life insurance that just expired. These two premises are the hallmarks of the buy term and invest the rest rule.

Let's consider a hypothetical 25 year-old, just married and starting a family earning $100,000 per year. The hypothetical premium for a $2,000,000 life insurance contract whose premium is level for ten years, in the best of health, with no bells and whistles for "convertibility" or "premium waivers for disability" is $385 per year for 10 years. Pretty cheap!

Let's stop right there because we were taught that when purchasing life insurance pay as little as possible, don't purchase all those extra riders. There is a lesson here.

The rider for "convertibility" is a provision that allows you to convert your term policy within a specified period of time, for an amount equal to the amount of the term policy to a permanent life insurance policy, without having to have your health rescreened for pricing and issuance purposes. Of course, if you are buying term and investing the difference, why would you ever consider anything other than another term policy?

Consider a few scenarios:

Scenario 1 – You are at the end of the level portion of your term policy. And the $385 is about to go up to $4,445 in year 11 and during the last ten years you have started to smoke. Your alternative here is take another term policy, but no longer at the best insurance rates once the insurance company realizes you picked up the habit of smoking during the last ten years, the new

10 year term policy is no longer $385 a year, but now $4,085. This is still not $4,445, but fairly discouraging. You choose this new policy, but you don't have much of the "invest the rest" money left. Additionally, after another 10 years you have the same decision to make and to continue this new term policy will now cost $18,365!

Scenario 2 – Your life has gone according to plan, however toward the conclusion of your last term policy at age 64, you are diagnosed with terminal cancer and you aren't expected to live more than another 5 years. You can keep the original plan in place, and surrender the term policy. After coming to terms with your shortened life expectancy, you realize that there is now a significant investment opportunity for your family, offering a better rate of return than you ever experienced in your "invest the rest", by keeping your term policy. If you keep this last term policy, having paid $5,985 for each of the last 10 years, the cost to continue the policy in year 11 is $61,965, but for a redemption value of $2,000,000 (a 3,000% rate of return) it is a good investment. If you live past the eleventh year, the twelfth year premium is $68,125, still a two year rate of return of 1,400%. If you live twice the number of years your doctor first estimated (10 more years), your rate of return is still more than 10% per year on average. The return might be great, but the problem it presents is complex.

- First, each year you have to reconsider your diagnosis and your mortality, even though you're are "beating it".

- Secondly, you will need to pump over $970,000 into the term life insurance policy and you might live longer than another 10 years.

- At any point after paying that eleventh year premium you stop funding the life insurance policy, makes the previous year's decision to pay the premium a poor decision.

- As you pay the premiums each year, and you live off of your "invest the rest" nest egg, what is the status of your nest egg?

If the original term policy had the term to permanent insurance conversion rider, the smoking decision and the cancer diagnosis, would not have been an issue. The rider would have provided alternatives that weren't available if this rider was not originally purchased in the original term insurance policy.

Lesson #4: Why what we were taught to be true about buy term and invest the rest that has turned out not to be true, is that there is both economic and emotional value in the convertibility rider of a life insurance policy. The economic value comes from being able to keep the level of death benefit for a set future cost that will never change despite health changes. The emotional value is in not having to revisit our mortality each year should we ever have to "beat" a disease. The consideration each year of paying another enormous premium alone could be hazardous to one's health.

The other rider that we were taught to avoid when buying term and investing the rest, was the rider that would waive the premium for the life insurance should we ever become disabled. Studies by the Social Security Administration demonstrate that a 20-year-old worker has a 30% chance of becoming disabled before he/she reaches retirement age. (www.ltdrates.com) A 40 year old male is twice as likely to become disabled before age 65 than he is to die (http://www.protectyourincome.com/education-center/disability-facts-and-statistics/probability). Given the previous example regarding the convertibility lesson, if that same person who unexpectantly was diagnosed with cancer, the disability waiver would eliminate the continual "investment" of future premiums until the eventual $2,000,000 payoff at death.

Lesson #5: Why what we were taught to be true about buy term and invest the rest that has turned out not to be true, is that there is also economic and emotional value in the disability waiver of premium rider of a life insurance policy. The economic value comes from not having to make continual premium payments during years of lower income levels because of disability. The emotional value is having the peace of mind that when the eventual death occurs, the hopes of future dreams will still live on without the additional monetary outlays.

Back to the hallmarks of buy term and invest the rest: buy enough temporary "death" insurance to replace the wage earner's income and invest what you would have otherwise spent on permanent life insurance.

Remember that the recommended minimum insurance for a 25 year old, $100,000 income earner is $2,000,000, and that amount of temporary term insurance costs $385 per year for the first 10 years.

At age 35 the premium on this policy goes to $4,445, not too cheap anymore so he goes shopping for another ten year level term policy. This time, his health has slipped a bit, a little cholesterol problem, that's all, and his $2,000,000 policy premium becomes $585, still considered cheap. But, we begin to have a problem; $585 no longer covers his human life value any longer, because in those ten years between age 25 and 35 he has gotten a raise and is now earning $150,000. Now his human life value is $3,000,000 and the premium goes to $835. If this were you, what are you willing to cut out of your family age 35 lifestyle, which now includes not only your spouse, but three children ages 8, 5 and 2?

You are now 45 years of age, you have one child entering college and two in high school, your income is now $200,000 and your term premium in year 11 is $14,065. Whoa – let's apply for another 10 year policy. The insurance company has now started to lower its multiple on you. Instead of providing 20 times your income, they will only provide 15 times your income; after all you were supposed to be "investing the rest". So the same $3,000,000 at one more reduced heath rating because you've become "too short" for the same health rating as before, meaning that your height hasn't keep up with your weight changes, and your new ten year premium would be $2,875 per year.

Now you are 55 and you figure you must work to 65 because you have to replace all that tuition you spent from the "invest the rest" pile, so you have one more 10 year time frame to cover. Reducing the multiplier to 10 times your income, assuming you have topped off at $200,000 per year, your last 10 year policy at standard rates since you now have added some negative family history to your personal health record and you find yourself spending $6,255 per year.

It is now the night before your official retirement dinner and you are alone with your spouse at your favorite restaurant and you look lovingly in your spouse's eyes and you begin to reminisce about all those years of working and raising a family. You tell her the plan has worked and all those years of paying for all that cheap term insurance has finally come to an end and that tomorrow you are going to cancel your policy. Today, she would get $2,000,000, tomorrow because you plan was so successful she would get $0. Hope you make it through the night!

Let's add up all that cheap insurance. $385 per year for the first 10 years is $3,850, $835 per year for the second 10 years is $8,350, $2,875 per year for the third 10 is $28,750 and $6,255 for each of the last 10 years, that's $62,550...for a grand total of $103,500. But, that is only part of the cost. What you are not counting is what you otherwise could have earned on that money had you not spent it. This is known as opportunity cost. Every dollar spent is a dollar that can never be saved or spent again, and neither can what it might have earned while in your possession. If we put the flows of money for what the term insurance cost over those 40 years in an account earning 6% (your invest the rest experience), you discover that the true cost of that insurance was $227,638. Assuming you made it through the night after you disclosed to your spouse that you were dropping the insurance policy, the next question you must answer is whether this amount you have put in trust with the insurance company is going to be refunded to you since they never had to pay out the death benefit. The answer is no, this money is not going to be available for your use in retirement.

Assuming you live to life expectancy, another 20 years, that amount of money the life insurance company didn't refund, continued to grow at the life insurance company at 6%. Your $227,638 has now become $730,067, surely that will be refunded to your children now that you have passed on. No. In fact, the insurance continues to keep it, and keeps it another 20 years to the point in which you would have been 100 years of age, the insurance company has the tidy sum of $1,749,649. An amount of money that almost equals your initial death benefit when you were 25 years old, and an amount of money that certainly would have served both you and your children well in all of your retirement years. All of this assumes that you succeeded at your buy term and invest the rest objective – you didn't die before retirement.

Lesson #6: Why what we were taught to be true about buy term insurance and invest the rest that has turned out not to be true is that term insurance is not the least expensive way to buy life insurance. It is a very expensive way to buy life insurance, when you account for all of the costs.

Human nature plays a role in this age old approach. The complement to "buy term" is "invest the rest". If you don't invest the rest, this plan doesn't work, in fact it fails miserably! All of the emotional factors noted in previous chapters come into play here, and usually somewhere along the way "invest the rest" is abandoned and whatever was invested is spent for things like vacation and college educations. The reality of "invest the rest" is that it doesn't happen.

Lesson #7: Why what we were taught to be true about buy term insurance and invest the rest that has turned out not to be true is that few people invest the rest.

As disclosed in the Rate of Return and Be a Long Term Investor chapters, the rates of return advertised in the marketplace just aren't what the individual investor realizes. Let's look at the trend of "long term interest rates" over the last 20 years:

S&P 500 Total Return

	Average rate of return	Actual rate of return
1991–2010	11.01%	9.14%
1992–2010	9.99%	8.12%
1993–2010	10.12%	8.15%
1994–2010	10.12%	8.03%
1995–2010	10.67%	8.47%
1996–2010	8.88%	6.77%
1997–2010	7.87%	5.69%
1998–2010	5.91%	3.83%
1999–2010	4.02%	2.01%
2000–2010	2.47%	0.44%
2001–2010	3.63%	1.41%
2002–2010	5.35%	3.05%
2003–2010	8.79%	6.70%
2004–2010	5.94%	3.82%
2005–2010	5.12%	2.65%
2006–2010	5.16%	2.29%
2007–2010	2.50%	-.76%
2008–2010	1.51%	2.74%

(*Source:* www.standardandpoors.com)

Remember, because your actual experience in the market is year to year, you do not earn the average rate of return, you actually earn something less. Not only do you earn something less than the average that is advertised, but you must pay investment fees from that and income taxes on the growth, assuming that you did your investing outside of your employer 401(k) or 403(b) plan or personal traditional IRA. If you did your investing in any of these plans, the taxes you owe will apply on all of the account balance; at whatever the tax rate is at the time you begin to withdraw the money from the account.

The eventual withdrawals from your permanent life insurance contract, if withdrawn properly, with the expert help of your life insurance agent will come to you without a tax. In fact, it will be sent to you in a way that is not even reportable to the Internal Revenue Service by either you or your life insurance company.

The benefits of proper withdrawals from a life insurance contract have a snowball effect. Because these distributions are not reportable on your tax return, they are not considered when determining whether your social security payments are taxable. If your only additional "income" in retirement is from your permanent life insurance contract, your social security will also be tax-free. If, instead your additional cash flow in retirement comes from a qualified plan such as a 401(k), 403(b) or IRA, that cash flow is accounted for when determining the taxability of your social security payments, resulting in up to 85% of your social security payments being subject to income tax at whatever the tax rate is that year.

Lesson #8: Why what we were taught to be true about buy term insurance and invest the rest that has turned out not to be true is that as evidenced by the last 20 years it is very difficult to beat the internal rate of return of a permanent life insurance contract after you account for fees and taxes.

Collateral Capacity

"There is something that is more powerful than all the armies in the world, and that is an idea whose time has come." – Victor Hugo

Many of the dentists that we work with have a large amount of cash value permanent life insurance on themselves and on key people in their dental practice. There will be many times during your career or in your personal life that you will need a cash cushion and the cash value of life insurance can serve that purpose! Once in force, this will become your "Private Reserve" which will be available for you to collateralize future purchases for your practice, use as an emergency fund, or just plain build a massive retirement fund that, if done properly, can be accessed tax-free. As it grows, you are basically building up your "collateral capacity" which will allow you to forgo traditional secured bank financing and set up your own unstructured loan (i.e., no structured repayment schedule, although any outstanding loan balance will reduce the death benefit) from the life insurance company using your cash values as collateral.

When we talk about life insurance, we are not talking about just any kind of life insurance, we are talking about custom-designed cash value permanent life insurance funded up to **but**

not over the government allowable Modified Endowment Contract (MEC) limits which will focus the policy on the cash value growth within the policy. The reason we want to stay below the MEC limits is that tax-free loans and withdrawals from cash value permanent life policies that are classified as modified endowment contracts may be subject to tax at the time that a loan or withdrawal is taken and, if prior to age 59 ½, a 10% federal tax penalty may apply. Your advisor will show you how to structure the policy and once you have the money in the policy, it will become the life blood of your financial portfolio while eliminating the need for many of the other money buckets you were told you needed in the past. This one bucket will do the work of several, and will give you liquidity, use, and control of your money.

Another advantage of permanent life insurance is that it allows you higher contribution limits than you might have with qualified plan funds while still maintaining tax-deferred growth, and your beneficiaries can receive the bonus of a tax-free death benefit. The cash surrender values and the death benefit will only be reduced by the amount of any outstanding policy loans. At the same time, we must be sure that the policy premiums are affordable because if they are not paid the policy could lapse or have surrender charges and we want to be sure that any withdrawals or loans that you make won't cause a loss of the no lapse guarantee, if one is provided for in the policy. If tax-free loans are taken and the policy lapses, a taxable event could occur, so once again let's be sure to consult with your advisor to be sure you are aware that the goal is to do this properly so you are getting the full benefit of this in the first place, which is to avoid all those taxes and penalties that you have with qualified plans.

Once this pool of money is properly established and struc-tured properly, it will never drop in value and will continue to grow uninterrupted during a recession or even a depression. Policy guarantees are based on the financial strength and claims-paying ability of the insurance company that issues the policy and it can be used for your personal use, as well, including saving for your children's college expenses. It soon becomes about the "living benefits" and not only the death benefits.

We've already shown you the advantages you will have once this reserve is established, but we are going to over-simplify it just in order to clearly show how it would work.

Remember back when you were 8 years old and started your first paper route. You probably only made about $22 per month so it took quite some time to save any money. Your goal was to eventually save $100 so you could buy this incredible Schwinn 10-speed, metallic-brown bike that you would go look at each week in the bicycle shop. It probably took about 6 months' pay, plus the interest, to finally have enough in your savings to purchase the bike. What a great day this was going to be and you may still remember it as if it was yesterday. So, you walked down to the bank and asked the teller to give you all the money in your account. She gave you the $100, you put it in your pocket, and then you went straight to the bike shop. It was absolutely one of the best days of your life to that point and the bike was worth every penny of that $100!

The reason we tell you this story is that on the surface everything worked out and you got good use out of your money as this was your vehicle of choice for the next 10 years while delivering papers, getting to school, fun with friends, and so on. But if we look a little closer, we would realize that you no longer had any money in your savings and just as you were building enough to see your interest begin to grow, you were back to $0.

You would have to work for several more months just to get back where you started.

Imagine if that $100 was still in your account and growing with interest while you had the use of the bike. At just a 5% interest rate that $100 would have grown to $776.16 by age 50! Once your cash value in your policy has been established and you have collateral capacity, you will be able to apply this same principle to all your purchases.

Lesson #1: Why what we were taught to be true about life insurance being about a death benefit that has turned out to be only part of the story, is because your cash value within your permanent life insurance will be there to grow and build collateral capacity so that your compounding interest accounts will not be diminished every time you make a purchase.

Lesson #2: Why what we were taught to be true about life insurance that has turned out not to be true was that you really won't need it past retirement age because you will be "self-insured" someday. "Self-insured" merely means you have accumulated sufficient assets that you no longer believe you need life insurance.

If anyone tells you that you do not need life insurance, ask them if they will provide a succession plan for your dental practice or provide the money your wife and children will need to pay the bills that do not go away at your death, let alone any college expenses or estate taxes that have yet to be paid.

Life insurance is the only way to assure that what you want to happen…will happen. It takes the guesswork out of saving for the future and it takes away the uncertainty that you have when you have your money tied up in risk-based investments.

All being "self-insured" will do for you is to put you back into a situation of spending your compounding interest accounts just as you may have done to purchase your first bicycle, stunting your true potential.

Your Home is Your Greatest Asset

One of the biggest threats to having liquidity, use, and control of your money as a dentist is the idea of prematurely paying off your home or the building from which you run your dental practice. So let's look at your home for a minute.

Even after the bursting of the real estate bubble, people still consider their home their greatest asset.

During the last 30 years, home prices increased year after year, and that growth happened regardless of what the homeowner/investor did or didn't do, as long as they practiced routine maintenance of the property. The homeowner/investor, because they live in the house, do not face the decision of whether to stay in the market or get out. In fact, unless forced to sell because of other unwise financing decisions, today's homeowner continues to "stay in the market" because the house represents their home rather than their investment. They are not experiencing the emotion of getting out during a down cycle which usually means missing the market rebound. Recognizing their house as their home rather than an investment is the proper viewpoint rather than their seeing their home as their greatest asset.

Let's look at an example to illustrate a few points.

Purchase Price - $220,000

Purchase Date – January 1995

Market Price (2007) - $380,000

Had this homeowner, cashed out of the property in 2007, the rate of return for the 13 year period was 72%. A great return, but when broken down, like we break down other returns to an average annual rate of return, that would be 4.3% per year. However, the homeowner is focused on either the 72% or the 4.3%, but on the increase of $160,000.

Lesson #1: Why what we were taught to be true about our home being our best investment that has turned out not to be true is that I was taught to focus on the wrong number.

There is nothing wrong with a gain of $160,000, or even 4.3% per year, especially when I consider that under current tax law that gain and rate of return is tax-free. It rivals many of our investments available today.

But that is not the whole story; the homeowner properly had his home insured for a loss that might be experienced through a fire, tornado, flood, earthquake, hurricane or other peril. In the Midwest (without the threat of a hurricane) the typical cost of homeowners insurance for a home valued like this would be $1,000 per year. This required "holding" cost of this asset brings the average rate or return down from 4.3% to 3.8%. I consider this a required holding cost because if you own your home with a mortgage associated with it, the mortgage company is going to require you to obtain a homeowners insurance contract. If you fail to insure the property, one of the pieces of paper in the stack of paper you signed at your home closing was an agreement that if you did not purchase the proper amount of homeowners insurance your mortgage company would – at enormous rates!

Homeowners insurance is not the only required holding cost. There is a little annual expenditure called real estate tax. The amount of real estate tax varies from state to state, but the real estate tax for a home as described in Illinois is about $6,000 per year. In 13 years this homeowner would have paid $78,000 in real estate taxes. Factoring this in as a holding cost drives the annual rate of return down to 1.55%.

Beyond the holding costs, there are maintenance costs. These are voluntary, but if you don't do them, your home appreciation will not be as described. This home was purchased when it was 7 years old, so in 2007 it was a 20 year old home. During the course of ownership, this homeowner/investor:

Updated the landscaping	$3,000
Repaired the property grading and drainage	$5,000
Replaced the Roof	$10,000
Upgraded the interior decorating	$5,000
Replaced half of the windows	$3,500
Replaced the air conditioning and furnace	$5,000
TOTAL	$31,500

Accounting for these necessary maintenance costs, the annual rate of return becomes .8%. Not exactly, the rate of return of our "greatest asset".

Lesson #2: Why what we were taught to be true about our home being our best investment that has turned out not to be true is that when we account for all of the costs associated with keeping the asset, the rate of return on the overall value of the house dives drastically.

Now let's consider the real estate market. In 2011, this home currently has a market value of $265,000. The current annual rate of return over the past 17 years is a NEGATIVE 1.5%, even though it is still worth $45,000 more than what was paid for it...certainly not your greatest financial asset.

Lesson #3: Why what we were taught to be true about our home being our best investment that has turned out not to be true is that we were taught that our home was a virtually riskless asset.

Closely associated with home ownership is home ownership financing. Homeownership financing is where the greatest asset term ought to be applied, however, we are taught that a home mortgage debt is bad and we ought to get the home paid off as soon as possible.

What is the least expensive way to purchase a home, with cash, with a 15 year mortgage or with a 30 year mortgage? Let's simplify the math and this time use a home purchased for $250,000. We need to also assume what the investor's best alternative rate of return is. Let's consider the best the investor can do in the investment markets is 5%. We also need to consider the tax savings of mortgage deductibility, let's assume a marginal tax rate of 30%.

Most would assume that the least costly way to purchase the home, if you had the money, would be to pay cash. That would be an outlay of $250,000. If the purchaser had paid $250,000 that would mean they didn't have $250,000 to invest any longer. Since we are going to compare this to a 15 and 30 year mortgage, we need to pick the evaluation period as 30 years. In 30 years, invested at 5% the $250,000 otherwise would have grown to $1,080,485 so the cost to live in the home over 30 years, paying cash is $1,080,485.

Comparing the two mortgages, assume the following

Down payment: 20%	$50,000	
Amount to borrow	$200,000	

	30-year mortgage	15-year mortgage
Interest rate	6%	5.5%
Investment rate of return	5%	5%
Interest expended	$231,676	$94,150

Many people stop the analysis right there and conclude that they don't want to spend as much in interest as the home costs. Therefore, only based on interest paid they decide to pay cash (no interest). If they don't have the cash they decide that the 15 year mortgage is better than the 30 year mortgage because they will pay $137,526 less in interest.

However, just as with home appreciation, that is not the whole story. Every year they pay mortgage interest. Because mortgage interest is potentially a tax deductible item, you must include the tax savings that they will experience. Furthermore, the tax savings need to be brought forward to the 30 year evaluation horizon at the assumed investment rate of 5%. When you do that the chart looks like this:

	30-year mortgage	15-year mortgage
Interest rate	6%	5.5%
Investment rate of return	5%	5%
Interest expended	$231,676	$94,150
Tax savings	$69,503	$28,245
Tax savings invested	$187,944	$98,029
Net interest cost	$43,732	($3,879)

(Interest expended less tax savings invested)

An interesting fact shows up here, in this example the tax savings invested for the 30 year time frame more than offsets the actual interest expended on the 15 year loan. In other words, over 30 years the interest expended is recaptured via tax savings and returned to your wealth potential. This is a very important word; recaptured. In every financial decision, it is economically advisable to recapture as many costs as possible as you accumulate wealth.

Looking at net interest only, you would now favor the 15 year mortgage over the outlay of cash, even if you had the cash. In 15 years, you would have completely covered the interest cost by the tax savings invested. But that is still not the entire story.

To get to an honest bottom line you must carry all of the calculations out for the entire 30 years, not just the interest expended or the taxes saved, but also the outlays of monthly principle payments that are part of your monthly mortgage payments.

Notice in the chart below, we have eliminated a couple of lines:

1. We have replaced the interest expended with interest otherwise invested. We have done this because

merely paying interest is not what is important, but what is important is what you would have otherwise done with the money had you not had a mortgage payment.

2. We've also eliminated the tax savings and more accurately accounted for the tax savings invested as described above.

3. We've added an all cash column, and identified the all cash as a down payment. After all, isn't that what it is?

4. We've added a line to account for the principle payments made each year on your mortgage and assumed that you would have been able to invest that at 5% if you didn't own the home.

	All cash	30-year mortgage	15-year mortgage
Interest rate		6%	5.5%
Investment rate of return	5%	5%	5%
Interest otherwise invested		$626,480	$326,765
Tax savings invested		$187,944	$98,029
Down payment invested	$1,080,485	$216,097	$216,097
Monthly principle invested		$371,482	$596,489
Net cost home	$1,080,485	$1,026,115	$1,041,322

The bottom line in this example is that the most expensive way to purchase your home is with all cash, the best way to buy it is with a 30 year mortgage. The difference is over $54,000 just in the way you purchase your home.

We purposely positioned the interest rates as close to each other as possible, in order to illustrate that the principle of favoring the 30 year mortgage, which most often is the best choice. Individual circumstances may cause the analysis to differ, however the greater the spread between the mortgage rate and the reinvestment rate, and the closer the spread between the interest rates of a 15 year and 30 year mortgage, the more dramatic the difference between your three choices will be.

Lesson #4: Why what we were taught to be true about our home being our best investment that has turned out not to be true is that we thought it was better to pay off our mortgage as quickly as possible, but just the opposite is true.

So what if rather than paying down the mortgage aggressively, you saved what you would have otherwise sent to the bank in a safe side fund? You would have the money to pay off the mortgage if you wanted.

Lesson #5 and a close corollary to lesson #4 is that it is always more efficient to have the ability to pay off the mortgage with a safe side fund, just in case long-term economic factors change the analysis.

Our conclusion regarding home ownership and the financing of your home is that your home is a place to grow your family, not your money.

The real opportunity if you value pursuing the best rate of return perspective comes from having as little of your own money as possible tied up in your home. This is because the rate of return on the equity in your home is 0%.

Consider two identical homes, one across the street from the other. They are both valued at $200,000. One is purchased with the minimum down payment of $40,000 (20%), and the other is purchased with a down payment of $100,000.

If the market value of each home increases $10,000, each home is now worth $210,000, if the homes are sold, who gets the extra $10,000?

    a. All of the gain goes to the bank, since without their money you wouldn't have been able to own the home?

    b. Shared with the mortgage bank since they own part of the home? In this situation the homeowner of house 1 would receive $2,000 of the increase, and the homeowner of house 2 would receive $5,000. Each increase representing the percentage of the homeowner's ownership.

    c. All the homeowners.

Since the answer is that the entire $10,000 is all the home-owners, the amount of equity in the home is extraneous information. Therefore, the rate of return on home equity is 0%. It doesn't matter how much equity is ascribed to the homeowner.

We were always taught to calculate our rate of return, on every investment. Even though we know our return on equity is 0%, let's do what we were taught, just to illustrate a point. In the gain of $10,000 on the $200,000 houses, remember it didn't matter how much equity you had in the house, all of the gain was the homeowner. But if you really want a rate of return, a $10,000 gain on a $100,000 investment is 10%, on a $40,000 investment is

25%. But remember if you could have purchased the home with no down payment, a $10,000 gain on a $0 investment is an infinite rate of return. You can't get better than that! If you really want a rate of return which would you rather have, 10%, 25% or an infinite rate of return.

Lesson #6: Why what we were taught to be true about our home being our best investment that has turned out not to be true is that we were taught to make as big of a down payment and establish as much of an equity position as possible as soon as possible. Again, just the opposite is true; there is no investment value in an equity position. There is not even a minimal investment value in the equity of the house. The appreciation of the home's value is not dependent on your equity investment. Either the house appreciates or it doesn't. If it appreciates the appreciated value is 100% the homeowner's profit, without regard to the amount of equity they have in the house. While we are making this point, the same is true for your dental practice. There is no rate of return on money used to prematurely pay down the loan on your building. You will also forfeit your liquidity, use, and control of that money which could be in a safe side fund. You could use this side fund as collateral to purchase a new digital pan or even remodel your practice or add another operatory. As technology changes and your practice grows, you want to have the cash available to use as collateral to make new purchases.

In fact, the larger your equity position, in either your home or where you practice dentistry, one can argue the more at risk you are.

Again, consider the two identical $200,000 homes. Not only are the two homes identical, but the family structure in each home is identical as well. A happily married couple, two grade school children, and both wives are radio personalities for the local radio station and both husbands are top notch reporters for the local newspaper. Their incomes are identical, and each income is necessary to pay the bills each month including the mortgages.

The first couple, Mr. and Ms. Hugh Debt, owes $160,000 on their home (made the minimum down payment) and the second couple Mr. and Ms. Max Down owes $100,000 (made a $100,000 down payment).

Assume further that both couples just inherited $90,000. What should they do with the money?

Ascribing to the logic of establishing as much equity in your home as possible, the Downs take the $90,000 to their local bank and pay the mortgage down to $10,000. They have bought in so strongly to have as much equity in their home as possible they have no other savings, other than in their "greatest asset". The Debts decide to buy a CD.

What happened to the Downs' mortgage payment? Was it reduced to reflect their $90,000 repayment? No, it remains the same; they will just pay off the mortgage that much faster, which falls right into their plans.

If Max suffers a career ending disability, what happens to the Downs' ability to pay their mortgage? It suffers a big blow. Will the bank give consideration that just a month before they brought in a check for $90,000? No! Will the bank give consideration that they have been paying their mortgage on the bank's biweekly plan and are ahead on their mortgage by 4 months? No! What do they care about? They care about the next month's mortgage payment being paid, in full.

What happens when the mortgage check does not arrive? The Downs are assessed a late penalty and their credit report takes a hit. What about when they can't make the payment in the second month of Max's disability – same thing. What about the third month? A foreclosure sign goes up in the front yard!

What happens if instead of a disability, there is a down turn in the economy and the radio station uses all national syndicated shows and eliminates the local talent? Furthermore, the economic downturn results in a housing value decline of 25%. Now each home is only worth $150,000. Who is in the safer position? Hugh Debt is upside down in his mortgage, he owes $160,000 on a home worth $150,000. Max Down feels pretty good; he owes just $10,000 even though his home has fallen in value.

The Downs are in trouble if they can't make the mortgage payment. Again it is three strikes and they are out, and the bank feels pretty good about collecting the $10,000 mortgage balance from a home worth $150,000.

The Debts are a bit nervous. For them it is three strikes and they are out as well, but the bank is a bit reluctant to satisfy the $160,000 debt with the sale of the $150,000 house. Instead of foreclosing on the Debts, they agree to waive the early withdrawal penalty on the $90,000 CD so that the Debts can continue to pay their mortgage.

Lesson #7: Why what we were taught to be true about our home being our best investment that has turned out not to be true is that the lower your mortgage, the more at risk you are of losing your down payment or any other equity you have in the house, and the safer the bank is.

How wrong is "your home is your most valuable asset" statement? Consider the following:

The 30 year mortgage payment of $1,200 per month in the above example would have purchased a 250,000 asset (the house) and would be worth $606,000 if the home appreciated in value by 3% without any holding or improvement costs.

If a 35 year old couple could invest the $1,200 per month in a permanent life insurance contract, considered by most a stable and consistently growing asset; by the time they were 65 and ready to retire, projecting today's dividend rates they would have $977,000 of cash value representing equity to spend in retirement and $2,000,000 of death benefits representing the bricks and mortar of a house to leave to their children as their inheritance. The guarantees of an insurance policy are based on the claims paying ability of the issuing insurance company which is why we always recommend finding a company with high current and historical ratings.

These values would provide a tax-free retirement income for the couple for 20 years in retirement of over $52,000 per year and still leave at least $1,000,000 of assets to the next generation. Try getting that out of your reverse mortgage!

We start our lives chasing the American Dream of owning our own home, our "most valuable asset". But when we understand the principles of this chapter we find out that "our most valuable asset" is valuable not for the wealth it generates, but for the memories that develop as we raise our families. Houses were meant to be homes in which to raise families in, not store cash.

Asset Accumulation

So you have built a successful dental practice, and now you are completely focused on building up your retirement fund. Actually, this process could have begun even before you graduated dental school, but it truly is never too late to start.

It is said "he who accumulates the most, wins the retirement race". Therefore, achieving the highest rate of return during your lifetime is the ultimate goal. Can you spend a rate or return? No! You can only spend cold hard cash. So at the end of your life, as you look back, would you like to say you achieved the highest rate of return possible, or would you like to be able to say you enjoyed the highest level of spending possible?

The goal of asset accumulation is like setting out to climb Mt. Everest without any plan to get back down the other side. Is getting to the top the ultimate prize, or is getting back down to tell about it?

Consider the following facts concerning the 29,035 foot peak of Mt. Everest. Between 1921 and 2006, 8,030 people set out to scale the mountain to the top. Only 2,250 of them were successful, a 28% success rate. Some would say that is a similar rate of success to those who truly achieve their retirement accumulation goals. That means 72% failed to get to the top. Most of them quit before the summit and were successful getting back to base camp to tell their story of failure. Almost 3% failed the climb miserably, not only did they not get to the summit, but they didn't get back down either. They died on the mountain. 120 of them are still there. Of those that perished, 15% died on the way up, they never abandoned their climb, and never came home to tell any story...73% died on the way down. They simply did not abandon their climb early enough to sustain the climb down. Now, the most startling statistic of them all: 56% of those who perished on the mountainside, perished after having succeeded by getting to the top! They died on the way back to base camp, after achieving their goal.

Just as in mountain climbing, asset accumulation is only half of the story, asset distribution is as important, if not more important.

Lesson #1: Why what we were taught to be true about asset accumulation that has turned out not to be true is that it is more important to not run out of money during my lifetime than it is to accumulate the most.

There are two ways to distribute your retirement nest egg. Remember that the money has to last two lifetimes for a happily married couple.

The first way and most conventional way to live out your retirement life is to take the approach of living on the interest only from your invested assets. This strategy is based on average rates of return, buy term and invest the rest and "Monte Carlo" simulations. A Monte Carlo simulation merely takes the market rates of return, mixes up the returns and looks at hundreds of random sets of return scenarios to establish the likelihood that you will outlast your money. Along with the random sets of returns, you test various rates of distribution.

Even a 5% withdrawal rate has a high risk of your principle decreasing. These last 10 years are a good example, because there wasn't any strategy that would have sustained a 5% withdrawal based on a 5% return assumption.

Remember this chart from the "Be a Long Term Investor" chapter? Starting with a $100,000 nest egg, and withdrawing 5%:

	Withdrawal	Rate of return	Beginning of the year	Gain/loss	End of the year
1999	-5,000	19.51%	95,000	18,535	113,535
2000	-5,000	-10.14%	108,535	-11,005	97,529
2001	-5,000	-13.04%	92,529	-12,066	80,463
2002	-5,000	-23.37%	75,463	-17,636	57,828
2003	-5,000	26.38%	52,828	13,936	66,763
2004	-5,000	8.99%	61,763	5,553	67,316
2005	-5,000	3.00%	62,316	1,869	64,185
2006	-5,000	13.62%	59,185	8,061	67,247
2007	-5,000	3.53%	62,247	2,197	64,444
2008	-5,000	-38.49%	59,444	-22,880	36,564

This illustrates that during this ten year period, utilizing the Monte Carlo suggestion, that 5% should sustain you. At the end of 10 years your principle has been reduced by almost two-thirds!

Even after you add back the market recovery years of 2009 and 2010, it is still not pretty.

	Withdrawal	Rate of return	Beginning of the year	Gain/loss	End of the year
1999	-5,000	19.51%	95,000	18,535	113,535
2000	-5,000	-10.14%	108,535	-11,005	97,529
2001	-5,000	-13.04%	92,529	-12,066	80,463
2002	-5,000	-23.37%	75,463	-17,636	57,828
2003	-5,000	26.38%	52,828	13,936	66,763
2004	-5,000	8.99%	61,763	5,553	67,316
2005	-5,000	3.00%	62,316	1,869	64,185
2006	-5,000	13.62%	59,185	8,061	67,247
2007	-5,000	3.53%	62,247	2,197	64,444
2008	-5,000	-38.49%	59,444	-22,880	36,564
2009	-5,000	23.49%	31,564	7,414	38,978
2010	-5,000	12.78%	33,978	4,342	38,320

Lesson #2: Why what we were taught to be true about asset accumulation that has turned out not to be true is that as soon as you withdraw more than you earn, the down slope gets very steep, and is hard to recover from.

Pretty amazing, because you would think that a 23% and 12% return would have reestablished much of the wealth lost in 2008. A good thing to remember is that the percentage losses in the stock market are calculated off of larger numbers, making the actual dollar loss greater and market gains are calculated on a smaller number minimizing the dollar impact of a recovery.

The reason why there has not been any withdrawal strategy that worked in the last 12 years is that the only alternative to being invested in the market is to be invested in bonds or CD's. Only 5 times during the last 12 years were 5 year CD's renewing at higher than 5%. Hopefully, you did not have a CD mature that needed to be renewed in 2011. The mid 2011, 5 year CD rate was 2.75%, and falling every week. If you renewed at this rate and were withdrawing 5% from your account, you would be falling behind each of the next five years. The only answer that the interest only strategy can provide is for you to reduce your standard of living by 45%! What are you planning on cutting back on? Travel? Medical expenditures? Entertainment? Gifts to the grandchildren?

The risks inherent with the interest only approach are:

1. Inflation - Since you are living only off the interest that the nest egg provides, you have a fixed amount of income. However, because inflation is eroding your purchasing power, you will likely experience a decrease in lifestyle.

2. Tax Rate - Since the government taxes the interest that you earn, you don't get to keep the entire amount of interest that is generated by the nest egg. What is the effect of the government raising the tax rates? You are still getting the same amount of income, but the government takes a larger share so your spendable income is decreased.

3. Interest Rate - What happens to your income if the amount of interest you are earning decreases due to changes in the economy or the interest rate environment? Again, you experience a decrease in spendable income.

4. Loss of Capital - What happens if either by choice or out of necessity, you have to invade your principle? Perhaps you have an unexpected medical expense or maybe you choose to help a child or grandchild with

some money. Any amount of capital that you remove from your nest egg will affect the amount of interest that you will earn in the future, which will result in a decrease in spendable income.

5. Market Risk- in order to compensate for the first four risks, people choose to put a portion of their nest egg into the stock market, which introduces "Market Risk" into the equation.

Lesson #3: Why what we were taught to be true about asset accumulation that has turned out not to be true is that there are major risks associated with living on just the interest my assets can provide.

Some of the obvious limits to the income only approach are:

1. The accumulation of assets is very important since at retirement they must reach a certain level.

2. Principal cannot be accessed deliberately for income.

3. Fixed income for life there provides no adjustment for inflation, resulting is a decrease of lifestyle, every year.

The alternative approach is one in which you purposely consume some of your principal with the income strategy. The only reliable scenario to this approach is when there is a guaranteed death benefit equal to the beginning retirement asset balance for both spouses. The permanent death benefit guarantees that the principle spent in retirement together will be replaced for the surviving spouse. At this point in life, the life insurance is more about insuring your assets than your life. Without this safety net, you lack the permission slip to spend your principal. Do not choose the "consume principal" approach to retirement income if you do not have this safety net.

(Remember that the guaranteed death benefits of a life insurance contract are dependent on the claims paying ability of the issuing life insurance company, so choose a highly-rated company.)

Lesson #4: Why what we were taught to be true about asset accumulation that has turned out not to be true is that there is no such thing as being "self-insured" with a retirement nest egg. There is a need for permanent life insurance in retirement. Perhaps better said, you will want permanent life insurance in retirement.

When the permission slip of life insurance is present during retirement, every asset is replenished at the first death, and the longer you live in retirement together, the less time one of the happily-married couple will live as a survivor. The longer you live, the more available the cash values are for consumption, allowing you to retire earlier, enhancing your lifestyle, or reducing the pressure on your accumulation assets to perform.

The key features of the consumption of principle and interest strategy are:

1. As you spend down your principle you have more money to enjoy your retirement.

2. Your spouse's income is covered with your death benefit.

3. The cash values of your life insurance policy provide you with less fear of running out of money.

Rather than having risks associated with this strategy, the risks associated with the income only approach are mitigated:

1. Inflation - when you have the ability to consume your principle, you can mitigate inflation by taking out less money in the early years of retirement and then in-

creasing your distribution each year to keep up with inflation. The effect is that you can level your purchasing power.

2. Tax Rate - by spending some of your principle every year you are reducing the size of your nest egg which means there is less principle to earn interest on in the succeeding years. As you earn less interest, you pay less tax. So, even if the tax rate increases in the future, there is less interest being earned so it mitigates the impact of the tax increase.

3. Interest Rate - when you are consuming your own principle, a decrease in interest rate has less effect on your income than if you were trying to live on the interest alone.

4. Loss of Capital - you are already consuming your own capital so, again, while it would impact your spendable income, you would still have more spendable income than if you were trying to live only on the interest.

5. Market Risk - you could actually eliminate market risk from this alternative because you could construct a portfolio that would earn 2-3% return without exposing any of the assets to the market and, because of your ability to consume your principle, you would still have more income than living off interest alone.

Lesson #5: Why what we were taught to be true about asset accumulation that has turned out not to be true is that while we may not "need" life insurance, we should certainly "want" life insurance, for the protection of our assets in retirement.

Remember, the climb to the top is difficult and quite precarious, but the descent is wrought with even more obstacles including those unseen and taken for granted as being safe. If something you thought to be true, turned out not to be true, when would you want to know about it?

What We Believe

We Believe ...

1. The financial decision making process is more important than any product available.

2. Every dentist ought to be out of debt – the probability of financial success is greatly enhanced if you are debt free.

3. There is a minimum amount one ought to be saving.

4. Every dentist ought to know where they are today – how are they are doing financially?

5. They are entitled to know if they will be financially successful if they keep doing what they are doing.

6. Many are transferring their money away unnecessarily – they ought to know where this is happening.

7. Cash values are more valuable than home equity or having equity in your dental building.

8. Your home and business mortgages should be paid off as quickly as possible.

9. Your mortgages are paid off when you have the money to pay it off, not when you terminate the mortgage contract.

10. Taxable income from assets that are in a taxable environment for a long period time has a devastating effect on your ability to accumulate money.

11. Opportunity cost is a real thing. If you lose a dollar, you not only lose the dollar but also what that dollar could have earned over time.

12. Qualified plans (401Ks, IRAs, etc.) defer the tax AND the tax calculation to some uncertain time at some uncertain rate.

13. The number one concern of dentists approaching retirement is running out of money.

14. Dentists approaching retirement want to talk to someone about the issues confronting them.

15. Distribution strategies will be more important than accumulation strategies for most dentists over the next 25 years.

Some Final Lessons

The Average American wakes up every morning to the abrupt ringing of an alarm and gets out of a bed that they financed, shower and clean-up to put on clothes that they have financed, hop in a car that has been financed, use gas they bought with a credit card, go out for lunch that they charged, in order to work a job and contribute to a 401(k) plan which they can deduct from income and which results in a reduction of their taxes otherwise due. Then at 5pm they get back into that financed car, using up the gasoline they charged to return home to a house that is financed and try to pay it off as fast as possible with the money they earned at work. As they pay down the mortgage they cut away at the very tax-reduction they have been working all day to achieve in the 401(k).

It is a vicious circle, which we have all been taught very early on in our adult lives, it is no wonder the Average American can't get ahead.

Besides, realizing that some of the things we were taught have turned out not to be true, there are a few other quick lessons that are derived from common sense if we just stop and think about them.

Capital Is Critical

Most people don't have a money problem they have a capital problem. They make enough money, they just haven't capitalized, meaning they haven't put enough money away that will allow them to decide whether to use their own money or to use someone else's money. Remember, every purchase is also a financing purchase. You are either going to use someone else's money and pay interest or use you own and not receive interest. Recapturing or reclaiming the interest paid or not received is vital in achieving your financial potential. This is a very important subject.

Average Americans don't understand how important capital is. They just go pay check to pay check and hopefully not spend more than they take in. However, our cash outlays are not as predictable or as level as our incomes are, putting us in the position of needing capital. The choice is either our own or someone else's. Successful businesses understand this principle or they would not be successful and be out of business. A business would never try to exist day to day, sale to sale. Business knows it must have a reserve or capital set aside or an approved line of credit from the outside to carry them through certain cycles of business. However, even some business owners don't transfer that knowledge over personally. We live paycheck to paycheck with no reserve or capital set aside. It's not that we don't have enough income; we just spend it all with little thought to tomorrow or the perils that await us.

It really boils down to whether we will either learn to be the customer of the bank all of our lives or we will learn to be the bank. You must put yourself in a position to have the choice. Then learn to decide whether to use your money or use someone else's money.

Most of our hard earned and saved money is in the two most inaccessible accounts. Our 401(k) plans and our homes. We put as much money in our 401(k) plans and get our houses paid-off as quickly as possible. Because we don't understand the rules, we are locked out of access to these stacks of money. When we look at our 401(k) plans we hope someday they will come out of their growth slumbers and skyrocket just when we need it. But if the market soars, what will happen to interest rates? They may go up and so would mortgage rates, effectively locking us out of accessing the cash stored in our houses.

You want to be in control of all of your money, and you won't be in control until you understand how important capital is. We start life using other people's capital and never learn to establish our own, because we are too quickly in the cycle of borrowing and too busy paying other people the interest they are due. If you were offered the opportunity to invest $10,000, but you had to have it by the end of the day, could you come up with it? Even if you could be guaranteed a 50% return by the end of the month? Your answer to this question will shed light on how well you understand the lesson of capital. You may have the money, but if it is spread out in places you can't get to, then it has lost its value as liquid capital.

Don't Get Discouraged

I recently watched one of my favorite movies, Secretariat. I like this movie because it illustrates the importance of planning our estates wisely. If not for the miraculous career of this once in a lifetime racehorse the estate of an entire family would have been wiped out by the estate taxes that were due.

However, watching it this time I was struck by the incredible career of the horse Sham, perhaps the greatest runner up ever to run a race. Sham came in second in the very races that made Secretariat famous, except the last, the Belmont Stakes.

It was at the Belmont Stakes that Sham had the greatest chance. It was the longest race of the three jewels of the triple crown of horse racing. Sham was thought to have more stamina as a distance runner than as a shorter race sprinter. Secretariat on the other hand was a sprinter and his value as a distance runner was the question of the day. Leading up to the race, as the movie points out, the last piece of direction of the trainer of Secretariat to the jockey was "run him hard, just don't burst his heart". Sometimes that is how we look at our investments, we run them hard, hoping not to burst the account, we don't know when to stop and get out. We burst the bubble.

However, in the case of Secretariat, he showed that distance was not a problem, and beat the field by an incredible 31 lengths! His heart proved strong, and the horse that came in second was not Sham. It is said that it was Sham's heart that broke during the Belmont Stakes as the horse lost to Secretariat by 45 lengths, finished last and never raced again. We must be careful who we compare ourselves to. There will always be the story of the person who sprinted throughout their entire investment career, and never looked back...an investment career as spectacular as the great Secretariat. But those are once in a lifetime. Don't be discouraged by spectacular stories. Fight the fight and finish the race.

Sprint Racing versus Marathon Running

I'm also fascinated by the label "the fastest man on earth" This title goes to the person who runs the 100 meter dash faster than anyone else. Currently that title belongs to Usain Bolt whose fastest time in the 100 meters is 9.58 seconds. At the other end of the spectrum is the Marathon 26.2 miles. If math were the answer to all of life's challenges to win the marathon all you would need to do is divide 26.2 miles by 100 meters and get this guy to run the marathon, 100 meters at a time. Obviously this won't work, and math isn't the answer.

The sprinter is done after 100 meters and can't even go another 100 meters much less 26 miles. A sprint is over quick. In a sprint you are always concerned with who is right behind you and wondering where you are right now. People look at their money in the same way, always looking over their shoulder wondering where they are now. A marathon is forward looking with an eye on the finish line 26 miles away. It doesn't really matter who is leading as the runners leave the starting line. Your money is marathon money not sprint money. For a married couple both age 65 it is likely that one of the spouses will live to see the age of 92 or more. That is a marathon! It doesn't matter where you are after 100 meters. It is not how you leave the gate, it is how you finish. Marathon runners just want to establish a steady rate of speed that they can maintain over a long period of time. It is not how you start, it is how you finish.

Cash Value in the First Year

Life insurance cash values in the first year looks much like marathon running. Getting out of the gate is not as important as finishing the race. Most of the time what is deposited as the first year's premium is more than what is reported as your cash value. Cash value only reflects what you can recover from the policy if you choose to terminate it prematurely. It is no reflection of its long term value. Therefore when choosing a permanent life insurance contract never put money into the policy in the first year that you are going to need to access. That all begins to change in the second and third years, when the cash value is at least equal to what your annual premium is. In the most efficient permanent life insurance contracts, your lack of liquidity is only evident for a year at a time.

Hypothetically, let's suppose you put in $20,000. At the end of the year let's further suppose that you get a statement that says you have a cash value of $7,000. It appears you have lost $13,000. Your perception is correct and if you chose to terminate the contract you would indeed lose $13,000, but as long as you consider this a marathon run, the only thing you have actually lost is the access to the $13,000, just as the only thing the marathon runner has lost is the prestige of being the early leader. Being the leader after the first mile is irrelevant, finishing first after the 26th mile is the objective. The only question you have to ask yourself is; can you do without the use of that money.

It is an interesting question, because we rarely ask ourselves that question when we participate in our employer's 401(k) plan. In most situations we lose access to that money until we reach 59 ½ years of age, and only if we have terminated our employment with that employer after that age.

Instead, pretend you can start the policy in year 2 or 3 and look at the cash values in year 2 or 3 of the policy. In those years it is possible your cash values can be equal to and greater than the amount of money you put in as your premium each year. Your cash value in the first year is limited for various reasons, including keeping the contract within the guidelines of the IRS' definition of life insurance. This is extremely important because compliance with the guidelines insures the tax benefits of a life insurance contract. If the contract falls outside of the guidelines, the tax benefits provided to the cash value part of the contract are forfeited and the contract merely defers the taxes due on the growth of the contract much like an IRA. There is a big difference between deferring the taxes due at some uncertain date at an uncertain rate than deferring the use of the money a few years. Remember you don't lose the money you just deferred the use of the money.

The reporting practices with respect to life insurance policies can be more transparent than the reporting practices related, for example, to a 401(k) plan. While additional information may be included, an annual report for a life insurance policy typically provides the cash value and cash surrender value of the policy. This information tells you the current value of the policy, the loan value (which typically approximates the cash value) and the value to you if the policy is liquidated. A 401(k) statement, on the other hand, typically provides only the gross asset value. Given that a 401(k) is intended to be held until retirement, the statement does not tell you what value might currently be available to you. If it did and if your 401(k) plan had a loan provision, it would only show 50% of the account value. If there were no loan provision, hardship withdrawal provision, or other provisions allowing for some distributable event, it would show $0 until you terminate your employment, become disabled, or die.

Remember that in your permanent life insurance contract, you are entitled to more than the cash values. There are death benefits your heirs are entitled to should you meet with an untimely and unanticipated early death. Another way of looking at the loss of liquidity in the first year is to consider the opportunity cost of this loss over the same time frame you would have had to supplement your estate with an equal amount of death benefits through a term insurance policy. Let's assume that you are a 35 year old husband and father of a young family. To permanently forgo access to $13,000 in the first year of the policy at 5% is $56,000 for 30 years to age 65. Further assume that the hypothetical cost for an equal amount of term insurance at 5%

opportunity is $142,000. Which opportunity cost would you like to incur? $56,000 that you will have completely recaptured in your cash values at age 65, or the $142,000 opportunity cost associated with the term insurance premiums paid to the life insurance company?

Remember you are in a marathon run, not a sprint race.

Accumulation vs. Distribution vs. Generational Transfers

Financial strategies are completely different depending on whether you are on the accumulation side of life or the distribution side of life. The most dramatic accumulation financial tool may be the worst financial tool when it comes to distribution. That is not to say that you should avoid the Qualified Plan, (401(k), IRA or anything you receive a deduction from taxable income when you make your deposits), but it should be used in such a way as to have options when you take distributions from this tool for retirement. The overuse of a qualified plan may result in retiring in a higher tax bracket, than the tax bracket that was used to calculate the tax savings when the contribution was made. Getting the money out in the lowest tax bracket is the key, which may be sooner in retirement than you think!

Furthermore, when estates transfer from one generation to another, another set of rules is set into motion. There is a bountiful amount of money about to be left to the baby boomer generation and distributions at death are different under certain circumstances. It is time to prepare and know how Qualified Plans, Mutual Funds and Life Insurance, just to name a few, are treated, and structure your ownership and inheritance rights now. How you allocate is very important. As an example, Qualified Plan money left to a charity in your estate is not taxable to the charity; however it is taxable to your children, at their tax rates, if they instead inherit this money.

In retirement and at death, it is more about the strategy than the financial product. You may have been product intensive throughout your accumulation life, now it is all about strategy to access it. The sooner you move to managing your money strategically rather than purchasing the hot product the better off your distribution years will be.

A Golf Analogy

When you start to shift your thinking from focusing on the best financial product to following what is the best financial strategy, you begin to understand that a number of clubs are necessary to play the game. In Golf, you are only allowed 14 clubs. The one that gets the most attention and is practiced with the most at the range is the one that hits it the farthest, the driver. The driver is always the most replaced club in the bag as we try to find the newest and best driver to hit it farther. Hit it hard and hit it far. However, hitting it hard and far is wrought with risk. Rough, water, sand and out of bounds stakes are just waiting for your ball. You don't always end up in the fairway, but it does go far. It feels really good when your hit the driver just right. The driver is great, but the best club in the bag is the putter. You use the putter on every hole, the driver is left in the bag on several holes, and is usually only taken out of the bag 14 times, if that often.

The pros know you hit the driver for show and you putt for dough. Master the putter and you will cash more championship checks. In your finances, the driver is your accumulation tool, but if you want to get the most money out of your assets you need to master the putter. Permanent life insurance is the putter, because it enhances many accumulation products. It can also save an errant financial start, just as a putter can save par after an errant drive. Obviously it is not the only product in the bag. You need all the others. But, you can't get through a game without a putter. Unfortunately, many of us try. Accuracy is more important than distance on the green. The putter is the peak performer.

Get Your Social Security in a Lump Sum

What?

And tax free?

O, come on now!

Most people become very disappointed when they finally retire and realize that because of the way they saved for retirement they are going to have to pay taxes on social security income.

By the time that retirement rolls around, most people have their home paid off. The good news is that you no longer have a house payment, but the bad news as shown in previous chapters all the equity in the house is earning 0%, and completely unusable. The retirement plan is to make the house the children's inheritance live off social security and your 401(k). Excessive distributions from a 401(k) require you to pay income taxes on your social security. Excessive is defined by the IRS as $32,000 for a married couple and $25,000 for a single individual or marriage survivor (2010 definitions). Excessive?

How do you avoid this unfortunate surprise? Let's say your social security income is $1,200 per month and you own a home worth $300,000 without a mortgage debt. If you were able to obtain an interest only 30 year mortgage, with 20% down, your interest only mortgage payment would be $1,200 at 6%. What does this achieve? If you use your taxable social security payment of $1,200 each month to pay the deductible interest only mortgage payment of $1,200, you would end up with a lump sum of $240,000 tax free. To be completely clear, the $240,000 comes from the loan proceeds of the mortgage and is a tax-free distribution; the tax on the social security income is offset by the interest paid on the mortgage.

The best application of this strategy is for someone who doesn't really need the SSA to live on. And instead of waiting until they die to give the kids the value of the home, they can give an early inheritance while they are still living. Why wait till death to give your heirs the value of your home?

This is just one example of utilizing a retirement distribution strategy rather than an investment product. This example illustrates the power of not leaving your wealth in your home, and all you have to do is talk with the survivors of natural disasters for it to really hit home.

Disaster Lessons

A natural disaster comes most unexpectantly, even if we live in disaster prone areas. Whether you are victimized by a broad brush natural disaster such as a hurricane, flood, forest fire or earthquake or you live through a more local disaster such as a tornado or personal fire if your money is stored in your paid off house your disaster may just be beginning. Don't get me wrong, I believe that your house should be paid off, but the value should be in a safe side account and you should still be carrying a mortgage.

Under any of the above disasters, assume your paid-off house is totally demolished. The flood or earthquake coverage maximum may be significantly less than the value of the house, or you have a financially significant deductible. If all of your money is being stored in your house, where is the money you need to rebuild? A $250,000 limit, will only rebuild half of the $500,000 house.

What if there was a mortgage? If the insurance maximum is still only half of what it will cost to rebuild, but the bank is now on a major hook as well as you. And the bank has major legal resources behind the insurance loss. They may not be able to work it out, but do you really want to have to wait for the insurance company to sort it all out. In a broad-based disaster, you are not their only claim. Money in a safe side account that could have been used to pay-off the mortgage would be available to begin the rebuilding process in a safe environment until the insurance mess was all sorted out.

What if it is your business that is destroyed? Now, more than just your life has been disrupted. But with the money in a safe side account and not in the bricks and mortar, you can be back in business and not have to wait on the insurance company. This way, employees are re-employed and customers have remained loyal. Money tied up is not very usable. Money available is king.

If you are forced to rebuild, access to the capital is a very comforting feeling. Unfortunately, too many of us have to live through it to understand it. This last statement is illustrated by the Mayor of Port Arthur, Texas whose home survived hurricane Rita only to be destroyed in the aftermath by fire. In his interview, he didn't say "Boy, I'm sure glad we just paid-off our house" instead he said "The worst part is that we just paid-off the house last month". If his home was a safe place to store his cash, why would that be the worst part?

One last example of having a strategy of coordinating financial products:

If you are interested in tax-deferred growth, it is available in more than qualified plans. What do you like best about your 401(k) plan? If you are like some you will say "I'm saving all those taxes". Now you know that is an untrue statement. You are not saving taxes just deferring them to the future at a time in which you don't know at what tax rate your savings will be taxed at. If you like tax-deferred growth, how are you enjoying your 401(k)? Do you have fond conversations about it with your spouse and family? What do the kids think about your 401(k)? They don't know anything about it? What do you mean that you are putting all that money in your 401(k) but you can't enjoy it for 30 years?

Why not put the money somewhere where you can enjoy it and it still have it grow. How about on the beach or in the mountains? Like to ski, fish, enjoy the outdoors? Wouldn't it be nice to put that 30 years from now money somewhere where you can enjoy it today.

A second home in the mountains or a condo on the beach, give you similar tax-deferral opportunities as does your 401(k) plan. Your 401(k) deferral is tax-deferred and your 2nd home mortgage interest is tax-deductible. From a tax-deduction perspective, they are similar and you are not paying current taxes on the income used for either the retirement plan deferral or the interest paid. The 401(k) is supposed to increase in value – is it? The real estate property is supposed to increase in value – can it?...perhaps more so than before, ever since the meltdown of the real estate values.

In what other ways does a vacation condo compare to a 401(k)?

1. At retirement both will need to be liquidated to finance your retirement. The sales proceeds of the 401(k) are taxed at ordinary income tax rates and the sales proceeds of the condo are taxed at more favorable capital gains rates.

2. At death both will pass on to the next generation. The 401(k) will be taxed at ordinary income tax rates and the condo will be income tax-free upon its sale, since investments receive a step up in basis for the heirs at the owner's death. There may be estate tax considerations however, as there is with every asset.

3. You are limited to how much you put into your 401(k) plan; you can deduct the interest on a loan up to $1,000,000 for the purchase of your condo.

4. With your 401(k) you get annual statements, with your condo you get annual pictures of your family vacation to review.

5. Your 401(k) gives you deferred enjoyment during your working career as you anticipate your retirement; your condo gives you a lifetime of memories.

6. You are locked out of your 401(k) until you are 59 ½ unless you are willing to pay a penalty, but with your condo you get two sets of front door keys.

7. If you use your 401(k) early, you are penalized; if you use your condo early you can not only receive immeasurable opportunities for your family but you can share them with your friends and your kid's friends.

8. In your 401(k) even if you don't need it, you have to begin liquidating it at age 70 ½; with your condo even

if you don't need it, you can always give it away to another family member.

9. Ownership costs of your 401(k) include your contributions to the account and the fees to maintain, and invest the account. Ownership costs of the condo include the purchase price and holding costs as described in the chapter "Your Home is Your Greatest Asset".

10. If for any reason you suspend contributions to your 401(k), you will still have your existing account balance subject to whatever market risks are associated with it. If you suspend your mortgage payments on the condo, you may lose the condo.

When you are planning your finances, think outside of the box. Just make sure to weigh all the advantages and disadvantages of your options. There is not just one magic product, but with your imagination and creativity anything is possible.

After Thoughts

One of the most difficult things to do is to describe somewhere you have visited that can't be described with words. Sometimes when we meet with clients and try to explain these concepts, words just don't do it. But it is more than satisfying when a dentist has embraced the concepts and has experienced the results so much so that they refer their colleagues with enthusiasm.

It is very much like having visited one of our great National Parks, whether that is Yellowstone, Grand Teton, Mount Rushmore, The Grand Canyon, Yosemite, The Appalachian Trail, The Great Smoky Mountains or the Pacific National Monument including Pearl Harbor; the experience is the same: Your words or even the pictures you take just don't do it justice. The best way to explain the experience is to take your audience with you the next time to go, and watch their facial expression and body language as they experience what you have been trying to tell them.

If you embrace and apply the principles contained in this book to your dental practice and in your personal life, you will have had some of the experiences we have had.

About Us

 **Sean A. Quigley LUTCF**
(402) 730-6505
Sean@lifescienceLLC.com

As a business owner and entrepreneur in Southern California, Sean realized the importance of a well thought out and implemented financial plan. After founding and developing his highly successful business over 18 years, he sold the business and moved into Financial Services as his chosen career.

Sean entered the life insurance industry in Oregon, where he was named Rookie of the Year with his first national company. Followed by being named All-American for two years and National Champion Agent, he earned membership in the Million Dollar Round Table, the premier association of financial professionals[®]. He was, also, selected to serve on the 2008 National Advisory Council.

Sean and his wife Elizabeth moved to Lincoln, Nebraska with their children, Chad and Megan, to raise their family in the Midwest. Since his move, he travels the country showing advisors how to illustrate the benefits associated with life insurance while empowering their clients with the knowledge to make their own decisions financially. Sean enjoys the mentoring role and his complete focus is making sure that any advisor who wants to succeed in this industry has the tools and support they need to make it happen.

Bryan S. Bloom CPA
Bryan@lifescienceLLC.com

Bryan began his financial career immediately following earning his CPA credentials and Bachelor's Degree in Accountancy from the University of Illinois. Later he earned his MBA from the University of Illinois Executive MBA program. His career started as a staff accountant for the State Universities Retirement System of Illinois where he eventual became the Chief Financial Officer. After these 19 years of experience in public retirement matters, he worked 5 years in an accounting firm specializing in private retirement plans, before beginning his current tenure at Chesser Financial, an independent financial consulting firm.

Bryan earned Million Dollar Round Table membership within four months at Chesser Financial. He earned the VIP of the Year award from Ohio National Financial Services that same year. In 2010, Bryan was recognized by Ohio National with their Chairman's Navigator award, recognizing him for the personal integrity Bryan exhibits with his clients and business relationships.

Bryan is married to Pam, his bride of 30 years. Their daughters Callie and Corrie are also married and pursuing their careers and families. Bryan enjoys the personal aspects of helping his clients make wise financial decisions and has spoken for a number of insurance companies at conventions and agent training opportunities.

Bryan and I would love to hear from you. The most rewarding part of writing this book has been receiving your phone calls and emails after you have read the book. We will always take the time to help you in any way we can, so please feel free to contact us anytime.

Sean Quigley
(402) 730-6505
Sean@lifescienceLLC.com

Bryan Bloom
Bryan@lifescienceLLC.com